Advance Praise for

Decide to Profit

"Leave it to Dorriah to take a challenging concept and turn it into something simple and straightforward. Every CEO will benefit from reading this."

—Jeanne M. Kuttel, P.E.
Chief, Division of Engineering, California Department of Water Resources

"This is far more than a helpful and illuminating book on how to build a successful business. With the cold precision of a skilled medical examiner, Dorriah Rogers has performed autopsies on thriving companies and on struggling companies. She has dug into their innards, and from her findings she has brought forth a crystal clear operations manual, showing how to diagnose the hidden ailments of a business organism, how to heal them, and how to bring that organism into radiant health. Flat-out brilliant, A to Z!"

—Paul Chutkow
Author of *Visa, The Power of an Idea, Reaching for the Stars, The Making of Constellation Brands*, and other major business books.

"*Decide to Profit* correctly identifies key elements of not just process optimization, but also management and leadership in general. The expert loop is a great insight, but so are the role of leaders and teams in decision making, to name just a few perceptive points. The clear, real-world examples describe and put into a usable framework behaviors that I easily recognize from my experience with many rapid-growth companies. *Decide to Profit* is a key addition to my short-list of business books."

—Karl Maier
Business Advisory, Doeren Mayhew

"Dorriah's simple, process-oriented approach will increase profitability and develop a dynamite culture of continuous improvement for you and your firm. Making money makes sense to me."

—Mike Moore
Alliance Manager, R&D, Dexcom, Inc.

"No matter your business, industry, or project—whether government or private sector, every organization stands to improve productivity and project success utilizing these 9 steps. I have worked with Dr. Rogers for several years on multiple projects and have seen these principles in action. In short, they work."

—Tracy Addis
Naval Facilities Engineering Command Southwest

"*Decide to Profit* is a gem. For our niche arts nonprofit I found Dorriah's approach to be effective and clear, with corporate and structural principles that translated extremely well to our field of business. At the core of her work is Dorriah's key understanding of people, the importance of the team, and the nuances of strategy and goal-oriented progress. I would recommend this book to anyone in a leadership position regardless of their field or area of business."

—Alexander Tseitlin
President and CEO, Eleos Music

"Dorriah Rogers has assembled her intellectual knowledge base, years of experience with numerous companies, and practical experience into this book. The 9 steps will give you and your company the tools and roadmap to more effectively reach better profit goals."

—Vern Kuehn
Executive Vice President at AECOM Engineering Company

"An engineering position at a Fortune 250 company revealed to me that the field is a fiery incubator of innovation. An incubator lacking the appropriate vehicle for sifting and communicating ideas to anyone who could foster them. *Decide to Profit* is that vehicle. It takes the employee from ideation to either implementation or truly understanding what the concept was missing. Now, as an executive of a technology-based company, I appreciate the importance of the 9 Steps from the other side of the court. It's a tool that delivers the best and educates the rest."

—Garret Autry
Chief Technology Officer, Autry Industrial

"Dorriah has put together a book/tool that is simple, understandable and had hits the nail on the head for dealing with direction in a construction company. I also believe this process can be used to deal with almost every major problem/issue we, in the construction industry, face daily."

—Ron Fedrick

Chairman and CEO, Nova Group, Inc.

"We were the fortunate ones; we met Dorriah Rogers at the height of the construction business in our part of North America. I only wished I had met her two years earlier. This book works if you apply it as she suggests—no short cuts and you will succeed. It takes a good market to make a good company, but if you apply Dorriah's message, you can become a great company."

—Greg Dixon

Deputy Division Manager and Senior VP (ret), Kiewit Corporation

DECIDE TO
PROFIT

9 Steps
to a Better Bottom Line

DORRIAH L. ROGERS, PhD

SelectBooks, Inc.
New York

This edition published by SelectBooks, Inc.
For information address SelectBooks, Inc., New York, New York.

First Edition

ISBN 978-1-59079-427-2

Library of Congress Cataloging-in-Publication Data

Names: Rogers, Dorriah L., author.
Title: Decide to profit : 9 steps to a better bottom line / Dorriah L.
  Rogers, PhD.
Description: First edition. | New York : SelectBooks, Inc., [2017] |
Includes
  bibliographical references and index.
Identifiers: LCCN 2016057137 | ISBN 9781590794272 (hardbound book : alk.
  paper)
Subjects: LCSH: Organizational effectiveness. | Organizational behavior. |
  Performance. | Profit.
Classification: LCC HD58.9 .R64 2017 | DDC 658.15--dc23 LC record available
at https://lccn.loc.gov/2016057137

Book design by Janice Benight

Manufactured in the United States of America
10 9 8 7 6 5 4 3 2 1

To the late Tom Schumacher, my mentor of thirty years.
I miss you every day.

Contents

Foreword vii

Preface xiii

Acknowledgments xvii

Introduction 1

STEP 1
Identify the System That Needs Improvement 7

STEP 2
Put the Right Team Together 23

STEP 3
Identify the Goal 49

STEP 4
Observe the System 65

STEP 5
Identify Bottlenecks within the System 93

STEP 6
Brainstorm 111

STEP 7
Select Optimal Solution(s) for Improvement   133

STEP 8
Implement One Change at a Time   157

STEP 9
Sustain a Culture of Continuous Improvement   175

Resources   193

Index   201

About the Author   213

Foreword

I'll start and end this foreword with a question because readers' contemplation of the 9 Steps outlined in Dr. Dorriah Roger's book results in a welcome self-discovery—they will find an answer to their search for the opportunity to improve their bottom line.

This first question is, "How committed are you to improving your company's performance and making a positive impact on the **bottom line**?"

Dr. Rogers' clear focus on the bottom line does not mean that this book has a narrow prescriptive approach. One might ask, "Why are there 9 steps?" Or, "What does this book provide that other dozens of books written on performance improvement do not?"

An anecdotal 2, 3, or 5 steps can be too simplistic and perhaps a "flavor of the month." Speaking from my experience of working with Dr. Rogers, outlining steps that are detailed and thorough allow the business leader to adapt and utilize these 9 steps for specific application to one's system or business.

What this book also provides is a call for feedback from the reader or a company. This reflects the willingness of Dr. Rogers to provide a process where she will engage with your company and provide great value, not just a consultation before moving on to the next client. After reading this book, I realized there were many similarities in the 9 steps to how Dr. Rogers proceeded when working with our company. Here's an example of my experience in working with Paradyne Consulting:

When we made a call to Paradyne over four years ago, we told Dr. Rogers that we had a need to develop operations training and also senior leadership training. We did not want a canned, prescriptive approach. We wanted something that was specific to our operating companies. She and Anne Marie Sullivan traveled up to help us identify the system that we believed needed improvement. For our company, the specific goal was to create an effective training program that was pragmatic, added value, and improved our bottom line. They both listened so well that we were able to move to step #6, Brainstorming, right then and there during our first meeting.

After this first meeting, we decided to move forward with the process. Building the right team, identifying the goals, and removing any bottlenecks all happened during our process to build our operations and senior leadership training programs. Reading this book four years after we had already traveled this road with Dr. Rogers reminds me of how we effectively used the 9 steps, even though the steps were not yet formally written as a specific methodology for us to accomplish our goals.

We did not implement one change at a time (Step 8). We should have. We launched both programs with a sense of urgency and we "got 'er done," trying to make up for the time when we did not have this training. Looking back, we should have launched one program at a time and staged each launch separately. This would have avoided training saturation and overload. Our programs have been well received, and the feedback is very positive. Training is crucial to strengthening our skill sets, yet it is one of the many other opportunities, duties and responsibilities our employees have to tackle during their work weeks. Implementing one program at a time would have been better. Lesson learned on my part.

The work Dr. Rogers provided for our company definitively helped to create a culture of continuous improvement (Step 9). Our employees who have been through our training programs are now more engaged and empowered to bring forward ideas and solutions to our internal systems when they see that improvement is needed.

Is this an endorsement? Call it what you want, but I'll call it a case study. Working with the 9 Steps from *Decide to Profit* has improved our company's performance and bottom line.

Pro-actively responding to changing business environments is crucial for the sustainability of a system or a business. Clearly communicating your organization's goals and aligning initiatives is a most productive venture for your company, but it does not start and end there.

Step 1 identifies the importance of focus and consistency when identifying systems that warrant improvement. Getting feedback from stakeholders, including those closest to the work and those experts outside of your organization, will guide the team towards success. This does not mean that a leader runs the company by polls. He or she has to build a team, which is Step 2.

Building a team does not mean that the leader abdicates responsibility to the decision-making process. It means that the leader has to do their homework first through a due diligence process. Which team members do they select? Some team members might have an instinctual, "gut" approach. This can be valuable, but it could also appear to others as impulsive, reckless, and unclear. Are they avoiding the hard work and facts presented by others because this might invalidate their instincts? Are they respecting the process of working through details and the 9 Steps with other team members?

Other leaders embroil themselves in details with the intent of analyzing thoroughly, and making an informed decision after evaluating from all angles, inside and out. Are these leaders avoiding making a decision, or otherwise looking for a perfect answer from the evaluation of the details that they are so closely studying? Good ideas and decisions that are not implemented in a timely manner lose their validity and can frustrate a team, thus missing an opportunity.

And, which of these two styles above is more apt to be a "talker?" Which one is more of a "listener." Both styles have value.

Building a diverse team with unique talents and perspective can be an incubator for solving system issues, blending different styles into a diverse group of thinkers, and creating a strong team that works collaboratively through brainstorming (Step 6).

The team has a duty to listen, as well as communicate, as goals are identified (Step 3), and develop meaningful key measurements for observing the system (Step 4), as well as to identify anticipated bottlenecks (Step 5) such that they are avoided or immediately shattered.

Steps, checklists, flowcharts, and processes are tools that when effectively deployed can build a "playbook" (using a sports metaphor) ready for selecting the best recommendations and solutions for improvement (Step 7). Dr. Rogers uses real-world examples with learned principles that can be pragmatically applied. Deploying these tools with effective teams will put organizations in the best possible position to implement the changes, one at a time (Step 8). Although many leaders, managers, and systems owners can become enthusiastic, and even impatient, about putting their work to use, too much too soon can defeat the whole purpose of the team's work. Therefore, even though intervals may vary between solutions, implementing at the right time is key.

The days of companies investing in a "one and done" practice, seminar, or conference are over if you plan to get your return on investment for systems improvement. You have to make it "stick." The byproduct of working through the first 8 steps is a return on that investment if one exercises a demonstrated commitment and discipline toward your system teams, and as importantly for a manager or executive, by following through with them. This can ultimately result in a sustained continuous process improvement culture (Step 9).

Keeping the focus on making money is the single most important takeaway from this book and Dr. Rogers' 9 steps can make a positive impact to your bottom line.

So the question is not, "What do you have to lose by implementing the 9 steps?" Instead, the question becomes "What do you have to gain for your business, employees, customers, and bottom line by following them?"

Enjoy the journey and don't forget to wash the top of that soda can!

—Jeff Thiede
President and CEO at MDU Construction Services Group, Inc.

Preface

A few years ago I was in Chicago with a client. We had just completed a series of long, arduous meetings held in a (too) small conference room. At the end of the third day I sat with a senior executive at a table in the lobby of the hotel. We were both exhausted and complaining about how (in our opinion) the discussions had been entirely unproductive. He asked me why I thought his company simply could not figure out how to improve, why decisions continued to be entirely disconnected from financial goals, and why both managers and employees continued to function independently with little to no accountability around their choices. I told him that we just needed to stay focused, and that if we were persistent and followed the road map he and I had discussed that we would get there.

He smiled and said, "Unfortunately that road map is in your head. I understand what you are saying and what we are trying to do, but I wish we had it down on paper step-by-step, like an operations manual for our company." And it was at that moment this journey began. I remember thinking to myself, "why not an operations manual?" If I could just combine all of the tools that I independently recommend to my clients in one single process, it literally could serve as a performance, productivity and profit improvement roadmap.

That very evening I sat down and doodled on a piece of paper, came up with a basic outline and spent the next couple of years testing and refining the steps. The checklists and forms were developed with a tremendous amount of real-world input from some very smart and extremely helpful guinea pigs. My instructions during the development process were pretty straightforward: keep it simple and if it doesn't work, dump it.

Over the course of developing *Decide to Profit*, I have researched, reviewed, and tested the applicability of a number of models. The ones I ultimately decided to use within the book were chosen not because other models were incorrect or weak, but because during my vetting process with real-world companies they proved to be the simplest and most effective to implement. I followed my own advice during this experiment, identifying improvements to the 9 Step model over and over, constantly seeking continuous improvement. Part of the beauty of the 9 Steps is that you do not need to even use any of the models I suggest in their entirety as long as you follow the checklists and the forms provided. For example, in Step 5: Identify the Bottlenecks within the System, it is not necessary to be an expert in the Theory of Constraints. While I recommend that users read *The Goal*, it is not required and if companies simply follow the checklists and fill-out the forms as presented, they will be utilizing the principles of the Theory of Constraints in their entirety. The same can be said for any of the steps.

The 9 Steps are meant to be followed in order. Each of the steps was designed with a specific purpose in mind, and each is linked to both the previous and subsequent steps. There are checks-and-balances within each of the steps, as well as accountability mechanisms for both employees and managers. This entire process was designed to be both comprehensive, helpful, and ultimately, simple. This is the first lesson of 9 Steps: keep it simple. Knowing where to start and following some straightforward checklists and forms is key to improving your organization's productivity and profitability. There is a tremendous amount of literature around each and every one of the 9 Steps principles (innovation, brainstorming, metrics, decision-making, and continuous improvement to name a few) and I have drawn liberally from many. I am a proponent of the "if it ain't broke, don't fix it" school of thought and I felt no need to reinvent when reinvention was not needed.

Within this book is simply a new way of incorporating existing tried-and-true models and business methodologies (a system improvement if you will) into a framework that can work for any business in any industry. I have seen this system work in many organizations across multiple industries, with significant results to the bottom line. What is unique is the ability for any person at any level to be involved in the success of the business in a way that can be easily managed and tied directly to the financial goals of their company. What was once a series of seemingly disparate models can now be integrated into a single holistic process that is trackable, measurable, and accountable. No longer does any individual need to be an expert in any one area. With a basic understanding of each of the principles, together with a clear methodology for implementation, businesses can focus on those metrics that matter. And, as I have reiterated many times over in this book: making money.

Another important element to the 9 Steps process is the feedback loop inherent in Step 9. Creating a culture of continuous improvement is the foundation behind much of what has been created here. Many of the organizations I work with express a desire to constantly improve, but many wander in circles trying to figure out how. I call it the *program du jour*. Which management book or new research are they going to try this month or this year? Which of the latest fads or language will they incorporate into their strategic planning initiatives? How will they reinvent themselves when what they are doing actually works and all they need to do is improve upon it? I run into this dilemma fairly often. What I think will make the 9 Steps process work for you is that you can mold it to your own culture and your own people, the way you operate. Customize the forms made available to you in downloadable format to reflect your own language and business goals. Assess whether the sample tools presented here work best for you or whether there is another model/

tool better suited to your organization or operation. It is the 9 Steps process and methodology that is important, not whether you use the exact same tools recommended within the chapters. The idea is similar to a diet: your goal is to lose weight. There is a process you must follow to do that: diet, exercise, nutrition. Whether you follow Atkins, low calorie, vegetarian, work out once a week, lift weights or walk, you are following a process to get you to your goal. I have recommended those tools that I think will get you to your business goal of making money just that much faster. These 9 Steps follow that same logic.

What you see here is not what I scribbled in that hotel room several years back, but the culmination of a lot of hard work and thought by some of the best companies and people in the world. And I am not vain enough to believe that it is perfect as is. There is still plenty that can be done to refine it. To that end, I am very much looking forward to the feedback and input from my readers. I want to know what is working and not working for you, within your business, with your people. I would love to do a follow-up with case studies examining how 9 Steps worked for you, and how you were able to impact your performance, your productivity, and your profit. Tell me how you measured your progress, defined your metrics, share your results, the reactions of your employees, if and how your culture changed. Please go to the following link to add your input under the Blog tab: www.paradyneconsulting.com/book/.

Acknowledgments

I owe so much to so many people who have helped me over the years both in formulating the ideas behind these 9 Steps, as well as the actual implementation and testing of the theories. First and foremost, to Anne Marie Sullivan, who has helped me run my consulting business for many years, in addition to serving as a sounding board and voice of reason during the formation of each step. Her knowledge of continuous improvement and lean methodology was instrumental to several chapters, and her steadfast commitment to this book and its accuracy has proven invaluable. She is the true definition of colleague and friend. And to her family: Jim, Kathleen, James, Sarah, and Ryan, thank you for putting up with all the hours.

I would also like to thank Greg Rawls for inspiring me to write this book in the first place. Without his original challenge, none of this would have occurred. Never have I met a more cerebral thinker who constantly seeks to challenge the status quo and motivate those around him. Thank you for allowing me the opportunity to use your teams as guinea pigs for much of this work. It was my numerous conversations with Greg that led to the concept of providing a manual of "checklists" and steps that linked good business decisions to making money, and I owe him a sincere debt of gratitude (and a Moscow mule).

Thanks also go to Glenn Kliebert, friend and confidante, who over the years has helped me to understand relationships and people, and how nothing gets done unless the people around you want to do it. Glenn is one of the best strategists I know, and his input about the value of getting people to buy in at the lowest levels served as a guide for several chapters.

I thank Fuat Sezer for the seven years spent together within your organization and for giving me the opportunity to be involved in your growth, strategies, and business decisions over the years. I have truly enjoyed our friendship and the challenges we have faced together. You are an inspirational and visionary leader, and your model for growth has been impressive.

To Michele Naame, thank you for making so many trips across the country not only possible, but enjoyable.

I would also like to thank the "Innovation Team" involved in researching and vetting the 9 steps. To Brad Dearing, who helped me with the early versions, your keen insight was critical. To Bob Shockney and George Osgood, thank you for reading the very early drafts. And to Garret Autry, Tim Greening, James Henry, Chris Long, Kevin Borders, Mike Myhre, Gabe Brandt, Terry Piper, Ray Longoria, Russell Quick, Wes Lowe, and Greg Benedict, thanks for all of the many months and hours of effort on productivity and innovation. All of you are represented somewhere in this book.

Thanks to Jon Swartzentruber, colleague, friend, advisor of many years. Your knowledge of behavior and how organizations respond to change has been invaluable. Your understanding of the interface between the consulting world and the corporate world has made my navigation in these waters that much easier.

Many other people are also represented in this book in one way or another. Vern Kuehn, Frank Richard, Ken McIalwain, JD Vetter, Vern Turner, Alan Alcorn, Terry Becker, Keenan Blunt, Sebastien Larivee, Trent Irick, Jim Austin, Tom Hawkins, Bart Dickson, Jeff Arviso, Kent Boden, Sian Barraclough, Doug Duplisea, Dick Colf, Paul Chutcow, Ken Hanna, Milt Plews, Mary Margaret Nichols, Glenn Stearns, Ron Duce, and several I am sure I missed.

And to my own team, Mark Sanders, steadfast and true despite his own challenges, Maryann Ferrari, always behind the scenes and just gets it done, and Arielle Williams for doing whatever I asked no matter how crazy. Thanks to Scott Wilson and Kristi Haar for helping to draft early chapters while still in the operations manual phase.

I thank my editor, Deborah Englander, for her countless hours of challenging, editing, polishing, and improving the manuscript.

Thanks, too, to Nancy, Kenichi, and Kenzi Sugihara for the untold hours of editing, assistance, and help in navigating this new world of publishing. Your ideas to improve this book have been immeasurable and I could not have done it without you. It was a difficult task to transition from a working manual to a final product, but your ideas and hard work made it happen.

To my friends Michelle Dotson, Keeley Mircetic, Jenny Christ Clark, Brandi Gentzler, Sandy Jocoy and Melissa Willie for their continued and unwavering loyalty in the face of many a challenge. You are my sisters for life. And finally, to my daughter, Dennesy, thanks for being such a great kid. You keep me challenged and motivated every day, and I love you more than pickles and sunflower seeds.

A Note to Readers

In an effort to provide the most thorough and readily available information to readers, I thought it important to supplement *Decide to Profit* with further details. This information can be found on the following link: www.paradyneconsulting.com/book/

A series of Appendices are provided within this link under the tab: Forms. Within Forms the following information can be found:

Appendix A: Samples of Realtime white boards as described in Step 1.

Appendix B: Blank 9 Step Forms downloadable in PDF format for your use and as described in Step 1.

Appendix C: Examples of fishbone, DMAIC, kaizen, process flow, root cause, and value stream mapping as described in Step 4.

Appendix D: Examples of Return on Investment analyses as described in Step 7.

Please feel free to add to our blog at www.paradyneconsulting.com/book/blog and share your experiences with the book, the 9 steps process within your organization, and any thoughts on the forms or the process itself.

Introduction

"Creativity is thinking up new things. Innovation is doing new things."

—THEODORE LEVITT
Marketing for Business Growth

In today's economy, the market is continually shifting and changing with clients and customers becoming more demanding, and the competition getting smarter. The ability to innovate and embrace change is key to successfully navigating this uncertain future. It is critical for organizations to be both strategic and mindful in their efforts, because doing things the way they have always done them is simply not good enough. Companies and managers have pushed for this innovation and change over the last few years, as evidenced by an onslaught of articles and books on the subject.

However, in spite of this battle cry for change and growth, businesses continue to suffer from net margin erosion, lack of productivity, a decline in employee morale, and frustration. Why? Is it due to employee ineptitude or apathy? Managers sending the wrong message? The answer to both questions is a resounding "no." Employees do care, and managers are correct in their message. Both groups understand what is important and why it is important. But neither knows HOW to do it. This book provides this "how": a process for employee-owned, sound and innovative business decisions that are the key to both sustainable growth **and** profit.

What happens within organizations as they push for change and growth? For one, behaviors change. Where once a handful of individuals made key decisions, these decisions are now spread across numerous departments and individuals at all levels of the organization. Agility and flexibility are replaced by process and a mind-numbing disconnect from business goals. Innovation and creativity are supplanted by overhead creep, loss of productivity, and poor business decisions.

I distinctly remember a conversation with a twenty-five year senior executive at a billion dollar company who said, "It's as though my employees have no idea that we are in the business of making money. Why don't they understand that the decisions they are making directly affect our business, and ultimately, the value of their own bonuses and stock?"

The thousands of employees I have worked with over the years experience this same frustration, but from a different vantage point. They see their ability to affect change as pointless or hopeless, as they are but a small voice in a sea of voices. Many have the *desire* to be innovative, or to contribute, but often feel their own internal processes and people make change virtually impossible, and many give up trying. The reality is they simply do not have the tools to be successful.

Over the last decade, I have observed many companies and projects (often in the billions of dollars) suffer from this lack of tools, and this has resulted in an increasingly wide delta between revenue growth and net gain (and for projects on budgets, the alarmingly difficult ability to maintain a percentage of profit the larger the project.) This trend is ultimately unsustainable for any organization, and I have witnessed numerous course corrections over the last few years. Most have been unable to get their arms around the wholesale cultural and organizational change required. Again, they understand what needs to happen, and why it needs to happen, but they do not have a system or process that ensures financially sound decisions that will ultimately improve the business goals of their organizations.

Decide to Profit: 9 Steps to a Better Bottom Line shows how to connect all ideas and decisions that affect change to the financial goals of your company. Employees will have a clear system that links decisions to the financial performance of their organization. Managers will have a ready tool to shape their organizational culture and business outcomes. With this system, both leaders and employees can adapt and change through external transformations in the marketplace and increasingly tough competition, and ultimately, maintain net profit.

This book is the culmination of the last twelve years of consulting and research for numerous companies of various sizes, large government entities, and the US military. The 9 Step process has been vetted and implemented within some of the largest and most complex projects and organizations across North America, and it works.

Following each of the 9 Steps will enable you to avoid common decision-making mistakes. The book also provides checklists and tools to foster a creative and idea-driven culture within your organization, and, ultimately, easy to understand and implement guidelines to ensure a financially sound future. The chapters outline each of the steps, its application, checklists, critical questions to ask, and easy-to-use forms for managers and employees. Imbedded within each step are checks and balances and a process for accountability so that managers and employees can remain in sync in both their thinking and actions.

This book is meant to be an applied process, not theoretical, and I invite readers to implement and challenge what I have provided here. I leave it to you to let me know what works and what doesn't, and, like any good system, provide me with sound and innovative ideas for improvement. Feel free to email me at drogers@paradyne-consulting.com or join our blog at www.paradyneconsulting.com. Let the journey begin . . .

— *The 9 Steps* —

1.

Identify the system that needs improvement

A "system" is defined as any operation, process, method or organization. The identified system produces work inefficiently and, if improved, will positively impact the business goals of the organization.

2.

Put the right team together

Ensure you have the right balance and diversity of ideas by inviting team members with the right mix of experience together with members from outside the traditional or expected network.

3.

Identify the goal

Identify a specific, measureable, achievable, and timely goal that will ensure that any improvements to the system will result in positive impacts to the business goals of the organization.

4.

Observe the system

Utilize the correct analysis tools appropriate to your system, include and listen to input from those involved, observe objectively, document and present findings.

5.
Identify bottlenecks within the system

Ensure that the focus of system improvements directly targets those areas that will impact the business goals of the organization most significantly.

6.
Brainstorm

Utilize the right team to accumulate a list of the best possible solutions for improvement to the system.

7.
Select optimal solution(s) for improvement

Ensure the best recommendations for system change are selected based upon thorough cost-benefit analysis, peer and stakeholder review.

8.
Implement one change at a time

Implement any proposed change independently of any other changes to ensure any measured impacts are the result of this change alone.

9.
Sustain a culture of continuous improvement

Ensure that the inertia of success or failure does not stop a culture of continuous innovation and improvement.

Step 1:
Identify the System that
Needs Improvement

"Progress is impossible without change; and those who
cannot change their minds cannot change anything."

—George Bernard Shaw

A "system" is defined as any operation, process, method, or organization. The identified system produces work inefficiently and, if improved, will positively impact the business goals of the organization.

Every business owner, manager, executive, or employee has encountered problems or issues at some point. Whether it is loss of market share, or an internal dilemma like a cumbersome or redundant process, everyone has experienced frustration in some form. In the consulting world, this is often the very reason we are brought in: to assess the issue and make recommendations for change. Our third-party evaluations can be valuable; we do not necessarily have a dog in the hunt, we do not have a vested interest in the existing processes or people, nor do we necessarily agree that their operations are effective and/or streamlined. Many times the organizations and people we work with already recognize the problems, but may struggle to clearly identify the problem and its full scope and then focus on this one problem when there are also other pressing issues.

This was particularly true of one large client that was growing and changing rapidly between 2005 and 2015. It had captured a large market share in the highly competitive oil and gas industry and was experiencing vast fluctuations in demand. These peaks and valleys were causing one-off systems (processes and project controls) unique to every single project, despite the fact that each of these projects was being managed by one organization. It was highly inefficient, not cost-effective, and was causing significant margin erosion year after year. Senior executives clearly recognized the issue, yet despite numerous meetings and discussions, could not seem to come to agreement either on the root cause of the problem, nor any defined solutions. Instead, it would assign business initiatives to "fix it," and fail. In my estimation, the biggest problem the client faced at that time was a lack of focus—the inability to clearly identify and zero in on *what* needed to be fixed, and not just how to fix it.

Finally, in 2012, the president told the group, "Guys, I'm frustrated. This cannot continue. Yes, we are making money, but compared to our revenue growth, we are losing money. What we used to be able to fabricate for a solid 10 percent return, we are lucky today to make 2 percent–3 percent. We need to do something different. We need to learn to be big."

While I have omitted some of the colorful language that accompanied that speech, the message remains the same. The firm could not continue along the path it was headed; it was not profitable, and it was not ultimately sustainable. That speech was the beginning of a long and difficult journey and served as the impetus for this system; for the next four years I worked tirelessly with them to find a way to solve this problem. The formal 9 Step process really began with that project.

Step 1 was designed to help organizations "start at the beginning." Just like my odyssey with my client in 2012 we, too, needed to find a way to start at the beginning. With so many opinions and so many ways to interpret what was happening, and no one agreeing which problem needed to be at the top of the list, someone somewhere needed to call a time-out and make a decision. But how?

The only way to make sure you are focused on the right area of improvement is to make that all-important link back to the business goals of your organization. If it will not make more profit for you upon improvement, don't waste your time. If you remain focused on the singular activity of making sure that anything you do will ultimately tie back to the business goals of your organization, only then are you improving the correct system. Anything else is an utter waste of resources, time, and effort.

Step 1 is the first and most important step required to actually get started, to identify what needs to be fixed, and to make sure you are focused on the right area of improvement. The checklist in this chapter, and the logic behind each question, is designed to ensure that you have asked all the right questions before attempting to fix anything within your organizational "system."

Key Terms Used Throughout the 9 Steps

You will notice that the same language is used throughout all 9 Steps in order to ensure both consistency and tie-in to all of the basic concepts. For ease of use and clarity, simple definitions for these key terms are provided below:

- **System:** Any operation, process, method, department, function, or organization that produces work inefficiently, and, if improved, will positively impact the business goals of the organization.

- **Business Goals:** Any outcome of the business that generates money. Other goals may also be included, such as safety, quality, customer satisfaction, and the like. Money must always be included in the list of goals. Other terms such as profit, productivity, velocity, and throughput may be used, but must always equate to money.

- **Boundaries:** The start and end points of your system. Without boundaries you will not be able to measure improvements.

- **Team:** An assigned group of individuals that will champion and implement improvements to the system.

- **Goals:** Specific, measurable, achievable, and timely units of measurement for system improvement that are tied directly to the business goals.

- **Bottleneck:** Any resource or step within our system where work does not flow to meet demand, and could be made more efficient.

- **Optimal Solution:** The best recommendation for system improvement based upon a thorough cost-benefit analysis.

- **Continuous Improvement:** Ongoing review and improvement of the current business systems.

So where do you start? How do you know which system needs priority? Begin with a list. Get together a group of people and list areas that you think need improvement. Any group from senior management, office staffer, or plant employee can perform this exercise. Once you have established this list of things you think may need improvement, you will use the Step 1 checklist to narrow it down to the "one."

STEP 1 CHECKLIST

- We know that this system needs improvement because we have identified a problem, a bottleneck, an increase in past costs, or a decrease in efficiency and discovered an opportunity for improvement.

- We have proven that improving this system will improve the following business goals (insert your goals below):
  - Profit (must always be on list)
  - Quality (example)
  - Safety (example)

- In observing this system, we know that this is the system we need to improve (not a larger system and not a subset of this system) and that we have identified the boundaries of the system.

- We have asked for feedback from the owners of the business goals that this is the correct system to improve.

- We have completed the appropriate amount of research and analysis to recommend that this system needs improvement.

- We have stakeholder and management buy-in that time and resources should be allocated to improving this system.

- We have defined a preliminary goal for our system improvement and realize this may be refined later.

- Stakeholders and management have selected a system improvement team leader, who is independent and unbiased, and this person will champion the system improvement efforts in Steps 2-9.

Each of the systems identified for improvement in Step 1 are processed according to the following reasons on our checklist:

We know that this system needs improvement because we have identified a problem, a bottleneck, an increase in past costs, or a decrease in efficiency and discovered an opportunity for improvement.

Sometimes we can rely on gut instinct to tell us when something is not quite right, and other times the data shows us the problem. In either case, it is important to verify factually and with hard numbers that there is an opportunity for improvement. Any place in the system that you can identify where flow does not meet demand (a bottleneck), or an increase in costs over previous years, or an overall decrease in production efficiency, is an opportunity for improvement. The simplest way to measure whether your systems need improvement is to look at the bottom line. Are you making the money that your organization is capable of making? Have you reached maximum profitability? Or, are your margins eroding? Are you experiencing increased overhead and reduced margin? Are you satisfied with your business results?

Keep in mind that it does not matter if the system improvement is something as large in scale as a complete reorganization of your business or something as simple as an accounting function, design step, or simple paperwork. Opportunities for improvement always exist. It is the awareness of the need for these improvements, and the desire to continuously make them, that will drive sound financial business decisions by your employees. An example of implementing each of the 9 Steps during the reorganization of a business is provided at the end of each chapter in the LEGO Case Studies.

Most employees and organizations can readily identify problems. They instinctually or factually understand how internal processes or functions are either dysfunctional or inefficient. However, most of this understanding devolves into long-winded discussions by disgruntled employees or rants by managers at meetings. Wrapping effort around improvement can be difficult when you do not know where to start. So begin with a master list. Then prioritize it. Make sure to prioritize it with those at the top that will impact your business goals the most. Then utilize the 9 Steps process for each one, independent from the others. Whether you pursue them simultaneously or sequentially is up to you, but make sure to keep the system improvement efforts separate for each.

We have proven that improving this system will improve the following business goals:

- ○ *Profit*
- ○ *Quality*
- ○ *Safety*

It is critical to **ALWAYS** align any system improvements with your organization's business goals. Otherwise, your efforts will be both counterproductive and a waste of effort. In this example the company is always focused on safety, quality, and—ultimately— profit. It is essential that any attempted improvements you wish to make to any "system" will directly impact these business goals.

I have worked with many organizations around the globe. I have seen many terms used interchangeably. Whether you use the term profit, gain, margin, productivity, velocity, throughput, output, or anything else, your efforts must always and ultimately equate to making money. This is the single most important takeaway of this book. Throughout each of the steps described in each chapter, continually check whether your activities and findings are aligned with your business goal of making money. It is a question I ask my clients on a regular basis. And I am continually surprised at how easily organizations can get off track. The methodology outlined here enables both management and employees to constantly circle back to this fundamental and all-important question. It eliminates many of the rabbit holes that many businesses spend inordinate time and money exploring. These steps also provide tools for employees to discuss and vet ideas with management in a time and cost efficient manner, rather than ineffectively brainstorming during unrelated meetings or "dropping in" while decision-makers may not be either focused on, or open to, ideas.

The process can be much more impactful when managers know employees are focused on the right areas and are pursuing changes utilizing the right tools. Employees have an opportunity to demonstrate that they, too, are focused on profitability and productivity and are vested in the future outcomes of their employer. This alignment ultimately results in simultaneous productivity and innovation, a combination that can be very elusive for many companies.

In observing this system, we know that this is the system we need to improve (not a larger system and not a subset of this system) and that we have identified the boundaries of the system.

When identifying the "system" for improvement, it is important to identify the start and end points. Otherwise, it is difficult to measure and quantify the effects of any changes. It is also important to understand the "bleed" effects of your changes on any other components of the system and adjust accordingly. It is useful to utilize a system or process flow chart with visually delineated start and end boundaries for clarity. It can be very valuable to keep this visual aid up for all members of the team working on the system improvement to remind them regularly to stay within the boundaries of their system.

There are several online tools that enable users to utilize and update a real-time white board. This visual aid can be very valuable and enable team members to review and update system improvement progress on a regular basis, as well as input their ideas at whatever moment in time they are realized rather than wait for a system improvement meeting. Whether your team uses an online tool or an old-fashioned room with charts and sticky tabs is irrelevant. What is relevant is making all data, ideas, and outcomes available, timely, accurate, and assembled in relation to each other.

This visual representation also serves as a frequent reminder of the boundaries within which the system improvement team should be working. It is both satisfying and fun to watch the project progress over time and observe the evolution of ideas and results with the visual tools. To view examples of this tool, go to www.paradyneconsulting.com/book/forms. Appendix A in this link will provide you with a sample of a real-world working board.

We have asked for feedback from the owners of the business goals that this is the correct system to improve.

Before beginning any efforts to change your system, it is important to seek guidance and feedback from those in-the-know about whether this is the correct system to focus your efforts on, whether improving this system will ultimately impact the business goals of the organization, and if the improvement of this system will have the biggest return for the effort and resources that will be expended.

Examples of those "in-the-know" might include those working within the system, (hands-on) department heads, managers, other employees, customers, clients, subcontractors, vendors, or others that may be affected by the system.

One example that stands out to me was a client who had brought me in to help figure out why the implementation of its CRM system was failing. The CRM system was costing almost three times what the company had anticipated, the sales force was not using it effectively, and it was causing significant frustration. The sales manager absolutely *insisted* that it was the CRM system that was broken. It wasn't until we spoke with the actual sales team that we learned that fixing the CRM system was not ultimately going to make the company any money. What *was* going to make it more money was getting the sales team to make more in-person appointments. When we fixed that (holding sales team members accountable to appointments, not CRM entries), that's when sales turned around. So the moral of the story? Make sure you are focused on system improvements that will ultimately make you money.

STEP 1—IN THE REAL WORLD

Client A (engineering and fabrication) grew quickly from 2005–2015. Larger and more complex projects were awarded by a blue-chip list of customers. However, along with the growth and ongoing complexity, came a creep upward in the unit-rate costs across the fabrication facility. Unit rates for structural, piping, paint, welding—no matter the discipline—were steadily rising and yard productivity was falling. This client had essentially lost its ability to build work at the lowest cost. These increases were not unsubstantial. In most cases, since 2006, rates had increased by as much as 40 percentage per discipline.

Senior managers were becoming increasingly concerned with these increases, and throughout the 2012–2014 business planning cycles, many discussions centered on the need to get these rising costs under control. In other words, the system that needed improvement was fabrication. In 2014, the boundaries of the system were identified by reviewing cost codes and focusing on those areas within the facility where the most improvement could be made. These included the piping, structural, and paint disciplines. Champions/owners were assigned to each area, and the productivity initiatives were established. In this case, management was not satisfied with the status quo and was not complacent about watching margin erosion despite revenue growth. This organization was open to the possibility that their system needed improvement, and quite possibly there were new and better ways to do things.

We have completed the appropriate amount of research and analysis to recommend that this system needs improvement.

Prior to seeking feedback from your network of experts and decision-makers, make sure you have completed your "due diligence"—the appropriate amount of research and analysis so that when you do seek feedback, you are adequately prepared to both present your case and address any questions. This is especially important for employees seeking approval from management to pursue ideas for improvement. It is one thing to have a good idea. It is another entirely to get it off the ground.

Without this homework, it is difficult for decision-makers to approve the expenditure of money and resources on the pursuit of anything outside of the normal day-to-day operations of the business. The key to getting this approval is tying both your ideas and homework *at the front end* to making money for the organization. Any idea or improvement is of little value if it will not result in a positive outcome for everyone involved in the effort, including employees and managers. And the only positive outcome that matters is making an improvement to an identified business goal.

Too often, I have sat in meetings where good ideas have fallen flat or innovation has been squandered because of employees not having done their homework. It is always a good idea to bring information, white papers, data, and proof. Make your argument clearly, concisely, and with back up. Practice your presentation. Run it by others before taking it to decision-makers. If the need for improvement exists, make a solid argument for it.

We have stakeholder and management buy-in that time and resources should be allocated to improving this system.

Another important piece of homework to complete is to ensure adequate buy-in and support of your proposed changes by all stakeholders and management. There is nothing more frustrating than coming up with an excellent idea, only to have either those who will be impacted or the key decision-makers kill it before it gets off the ground. Additionally, when preparing your case, make sure you have requested (and received approval for) adequate personnel, time, and resources to accomplish your task.

Keep in mind that managers and executives typically operate within set budgets and manpower allocations. It will be your job to present an argument in support of spending additional time and resources on something they have not budgeted for. This can be an uphill battle, so be prepared. (We will discuss how to do this in more detail in later steps when we discuss the Return-on-Investment analysis).

One manufacturing client I worked with had a particular manager who was notorious for saying "no." It didn't matter what idea you had, whether it made perfect sense or not, he would send his employees away with a "didn't do your homework, did ya?"

His team would walk away deflated, and after time they stopped bringing him any ideas at all. The division suffered, morale declined, and productivity waned.

Finally, as a last desperate attempt on my part, I asked this manager to explain exactly what he meant by "do your homework." After working together for several months, we developed a clear guideline for his employees: one that included both quantitative and qualitative analysis and a clear definitive tie to how it would make his division money. The manager understood the upfront costs, the risks, and how it would pay off in the end. The manager was happy, the employees had clear expectations, morale improved, and productivity began to increase.

We have defined a preliminary goal for our system improvement and realize this may be refined later.

Providing a preliminary definition of what you hope to accomplish by improving your system is key to obtaining management and stakeholder buy-in. The ability to articulate this in a single, simple sentence can be both effective and influential. Keep in mind that this definition may (and should) change and become more refined once the system improvement team is assembled and have challenged, discussed, and redefined the parameters of the system improvement goal in Step 3.

Several times over the last few years, I have worked with teams that set out to improve one system and then found out during later steps that they had to either adjust the preliminary goal, or change course entirely. This is absolutely fine. Throughout the course of system improvement, you want to make continuous checks against the primary focus of increasing profit at the end of the day. If, at any point during your examination you find that is no longer the case, then you must abandon your original goal and refocus on a system or goal that meets that requirement.

Stakeholders and management have selected a system improvement team leader who is independent and unbiased, and this person will champion the system improvement efforts in Steps 2–9.

It is important to select a team leader to champion the improvement effort early in the process. In some instances, the person suggesting the system improvement may be nominated for this effort, and in some cases, he may not. Either way, the selection process is important because this person will ultimately be responsible to affect change and carry the ball to the goal line.

It is critical that this person NOT be an owner of the system, but an independent, objective decision-maker who will make decisions based upon the merits of the findings and not from any personal or organizational bias.

Go to www.Paradyneconsulting.com/book/forms to download both blank forms for your use and samples of completed forms that are designed to ensure you follow all steps set forth in each chapter. Appendix B in this link will provide you with blank Step 1–9 forms, as well as examples of completed forms to guide you through the process.

The LEGO Case Study According to Step 1:
Identify the System That Needs Improvement

IN ORDER TO UNDERSTAND the importance of each of these 9 Steps, within each chapter we will review them in relation to the important 2013 LEGO Case Study performed by John Ashcroft as part of the Manchester Business School International MBA program. We will analyze the turnaround of LEGO as presented by Ashcroft, and determine its applicability to the 9 Steps presented here.

In 2003 and 2004, the Danish toy manufacturer LEGO reported that sales had fallen by 26 percent, and that they had lost significant margin across all sectors of the company (retail, parks, and brand stores). Given the significant financial problems, Jorgen Vig Knudstorp, head of strategic development, was asked to review the issues and report to the Board of Directors. In his report, he stated the company had lost 40 percent of its sales, thus producing record losses and negative cash flow. In sum, the system that needed improvement was the entire LEGO organization.

Step 1	SYSTEM IMPROVEMENT IDENTIFICATION FORM
Name of system that needs improvement	▶
This system was chosen because:	▶
Boundaries of system: (start & end pts)	▶
System flow chart: (start & end pts)	▶
Business goals impacted: Profit:	▶
Quality:	▶
Safety:	▶

BUSINESS GOAL OWNERS:

NAME	EMAIL	PHONE
▶		
▶		
▶		

Research completed to date to identify that this system requires improvement:

▶

Goal of system improvement (one sentence):

▶

Stakeholders consulted: ▶	Management approval: ▶
▶	Proposed completion date:
System improvement team leader: ▶	Signature Date

Step 2:
Put the Right Team Together

"Problems can become opportunities when
the right people come together."

—Robert South

Ensure that you have the right balance and diversity of ideas by invit-ing team members with the right mix of experience together with mem-bers from outside the traditional or expected network.

While it may seem overly simple, putting the right team of people together to improve your system is actually both complex and occa-sionally problematic. Cultural and political influences can often sway both membership and outcomes, and finding the right balance and diversity of ideas is critical to a successful effort. Your team should embody the correct mix of both experience and unbiased perspective, with members who are also invited from outside your traditional or expected network.

In many instances, the culture of an organization can directly influence both the volume and content of innovation. Studies of prim-itive peoples indicate that social interactions are central to informa-tion-gathering and decision-making. In fact, almost all decisions affecting groups are made in social situations. As long as diverse and successful strategies are implemented, societies thrive.

Business organizations are no different. Learning from the suc-cesses and failures of others, frequently and in a range of situations, is key to sustainable growth. According to researcher Alex "Sandy"

Pentland in his article "Beyond the Echo Chamber" published in *Harvard Business*, November 2013,* in his studies of dozens of organizations he found that the number of opportunities for social learning (which usually involve informal face-to-face interactions among employees) is the **single largest** factor in company productivity.

So why do organizations often create a culture that stifles innovation or autonomous decision making?

> ○ **The Expert Loop**—Within an organization, often a handful of individuals are viewed as the "experts" and are the only ones either allowed to or considered capable of making decisions. In fact, seeking information outside of the expert network is often more valuable.

Time and time again I have seen the phenomenon of top executives sitting in rooms with the same small group of people as they rehash both problems and ideas in a tired, circular rhythm. Even when new people are brought into the conversation, their ideas are often dismissed or even scoffed at, as the experts re-establish their positions of authority at the top of the food chain. While it is true that experts do (and should) have great ideas, it often requires a fresh perspective or a dissenting voice to shake things up and move the company in a new direction. This concept is discussed in detail in *Blue Ocean Strategy* by W. Chan Kim and Rene Mauborgne and includes a discussion on overcoming organizational hurdles. In sum, companies must abandon these tired conversations and not allow status quo to dominate the day. Instead, you shouldn't be limited by a perceived lack of ideas; they are out there—you must simply listen.

Second, just because an idea is new does not mean it must be expensive. Much of the reasoning behind these 9 Steps was to provide an ROI tool to determine costs early in the process, so do not let fear of limited resources or increased capital expenditures constrain

---

* The information in this chapter about learning from the success and failures of others in an organization is derived from Alex Pentland's article titled "Beyond the Echo Chamber," published November, 2013 in *Harvard Business Review* and is used with permission given by HBR. Copyright © 2013 by the Harvard Business School Publishing Corporation; all right reserved.

the thought process. Third, when an Expert Loop exists, it destroys the motivation of those around it. Expert Loops can be perceived as organizational black holes, sucking the light and energy out of any employee who enters.

For example, in a meeting a senior female executive told one of her employees that the idea for an advanced packaging concept would not work because "we do not have the tooling for that type of product." Wait. What? You are limiting potential increased market share and product innovation because of an equipment constraint? That is the type of thinking typical of an Expert Loop: limited in creativity, mired in past processes and clearly closed to new ideas.

○ **Overestimated Value**—Experts, authority figures and tenured employees all tend to sway opinion. Those without this status tend to be undervalued and often do not speak up. When making decisions, it is best to remove any value judgments with regard to information.

This problem is especially prevalent in meetings. I have seen teams of employees put their blood, sweat, and tears into a presentation only to have it sliced to ribbons in a matter of seconds with one sentence by one senior manager. In some cases, this manager may or may not have even truly paid attention to the presentation. This type of behavior not only demoralizes employees but provides fodder for an ongoing (and destructive) gripe current within the organization.

I often recommend that my clients hold important strategic and thought meetings off-site and away from traditional conference rooms or offices. I have observed these new environments changing the traditional dynamics of well-established teams, and the willingness of experts to listen to less-tenured employees improve. Whatever the reason for this, these off-site meetings can often generate not only new and fresh ideas but can also help develop camaraderie among both senior and less-seasoned employees. In most cases, these newfound relationships often translate into improved innovation and collaboration once the teams return to the office.

○ *Underestimated Value*—Non-status groups such as newer or younger employees or even those unfamiliar with the system can often provide a unique and valuable perspective. Make sure not to discount information that may come from a non-traditional source. In business, these sources and ideas can often be game-changers.

I had worked with one client, a large termite and pest control company, for several years. We had tackled increased market share, improved customer satisfaction and profit margins with vigor. The firm was a steady and reliable organization, and as you might imagine, it was tough to find further innovative ways to kill bugs. Or so we thought.

One young inspector had a head full of ideas and had gained a reputation for carrying around so many crazy concepts that many questioned whether or not he was actually doing his job. He tried multiple times to give a presentation to the senior executives on his new and fresh approaches to bug control, but because he had no perceived value within the organization, many dismissed his input.

So he left, got a loan from his father-in-law, and proceeded to change the termite industry by treating homes with nontoxic orange oil. His idea to eliminate tenting and the need for families to move out of the house for days at a time, coupled with the side effect of killing off plants and (potentially) pets, resonated with the public. He eventually took a large percentage of the traditional termite market away from his previous employer and ended up running a very successful organization. Had the Expert Loop recognized his Underestimated Value, things could have turned out quite differently.

○ *Personal Prejudice*—We frequently only hear what we want to hear and see what we want to see. If you have expectations or biases, this will influence the outcome. Be aware of your own prejudices and stay open to unexpected sources and content.

The older we become, the more we think we know. It is easy to believe that due to our experience, we have seen what there is to see, or that we have already tried all of the new ideas and concepts at one time or another. I have personally suffered from this disease. I distinctly remember overhearing a hallway conversation between two young employees at a strategic planning meeting in 2011. The young male employee was telling the young female employee that the planning process we were using was "the same thing we do every year and no wonder nothing new ever happens." That really shook me up. This was my wheelhouse they were talking about. I was getting tired? Clichéd? How was that adding any value to my client?

So I decided I should adapt. My planning "system" needed improvement. I told those two young employees that I had overheard them (boy, were they embarrassed) and that I sincerely wanted their ideas on how to change it and make it better, not only for them but for their company. I think at first they both thought I was making noise and had zero intention of actually doing anything differently. But I kept at it through the year, following up with questions, asking them to go to their cohorts and get further input, really pushing myself away from my personal prejudice over what had worked in the planning process in the past and how I had a "system" that worked for me.

The end result was a vastly different planning process the following year. Instead of having the Expert Loop present their updates on the previous year's performance and ideas for the upcoming year, I asked the Gen Y group to come up with one idea that could potentially change their company, present the idea to the Expert Loop at that year's planning session, get feedback, then return at the end of the planning process with a final plan of action.

Their idea was pretty fantastic, and their homework on the ROI was impressive. They decided that rather than sending their labor force to outside training, they would establish their own internal technical institute, a place where they would provide hands-on technical training to their workers using their own internal senior labor. This small group of twentysomething employees all committed to management to spend their own time developing the curriculum and pulling together the content. They assured senior management that the only effort they needed from the Expert Loop was final approval. Their math showed senior executives that the program would pay for itself in less than two years, and predicted that retention would improve for several labor categories. By the end of the planning session, the senior executives were completely energized. They felt the young employees really cared about the future of the company, and the Gen Y employees felt that their voices had been heard and their ideas valued. They were *vested*.

As a side note, that technical institute has been in place now for several years and has led to careers for the group of young employees spearheading it. Their idea gained so much traction and attention that several other divisions within their organization copied their footprint. The idea paid for itself in about two years and the company is now saving several million dollars in training costs and improved employee retention every year.

> ○ **Gut Instinct**—A great deal of information is stored in our subconscious. In moments of decision-making, our bodies provide clues to answers through feelings or gut reactions (for a fascinating book on this subject, see Malcolm Gladwell's *Blink*). Tune into your intuition—your decisions will be sounder.

STEP 2—IN THE REAL WORLD

Client A had to do something. Management recognized the problem and agreed that a solution was critical (Step 1: Real World). One of the first areas they tackled was structural assembly. So a champion was assigned to fix it. Don, a lead engineer, realized early on that the team he assembled to tackle this issue was a critical component to his success. He sat with several people to brainstorm on who might be the right people for his team. As he assembled this group, together they realized they needed new blood, new voices, ideas that had not already been heard. The team brought in experts, guys who did the actual work in the field, consultants, job superintendents, craft, people who actually built the work, as well as some younger engineers. The group actively sought input from outside the expected network of people. In other words, they avoided the same people discussing the very same problems over and over (the echo chamber).

This time they tackled the problem with a fresh set of eyes and some typically quiet voices. This new group met on a regular basis to address the issue of improvement, and over the course of their efforts, found that they grew to respect the diversity of ideas and each other. This group of individuals felt empowered, and as their ideas gained momentum, they began to feed from their successes. The teamwork and camaraderie led to further improvements, and team members found themselves offering previously unthought-of solutions, and ultimately receiving accolades for their successful implementation. The single most effective idea for implementation ended up coming from a guy in the field, who single-handedly ended up improving productivity in his area over 60 percent.

Everyone has those moments when the answer just seems to magically pop into your head, or the solution is obvious. The same can be said for change and innovation. Often, individuals just seem to *know* when something is off, or alternatively when a system improvement is obvious. So why is this instinct so often ignored? Why do teams revert back to old ideas and behaviors so readily? I believe much of this has to do with the second-guessing of our own (or others') instinctual decisions and reversion back to Expert Loops, Overestimated Value, and Personal Prejudice. For example, how can I know the answer when *the expert* says otherwise? How is his idea any good if *I* have experienced only the opposite? These types of internal dialogues are common among employees who are either dismissed as noncontributors or leaders typically not open to the concept that brainstorming atypical ideas can actually be a good thing, that inviting people outside of your expected network can add value to the discussion.

Next time someone blurts out one of those a-ha moments, listen. Take notes. Vet the idea, not the person offering it. The composition of the teams that will tackle your system improvements is absolutely critical to your success. Make sure you have considered whether the system improvement team consists only of those in the Expert Loop or with Overestimated Value. If it is, you are missing out on the possibility of exponential change for the good. Invite both the experts and the inexperienced, the ancillary, the vested, the customer, the manufacturer, the consultant, the boss—anyone who can add value to the discussion. Innovation and improvement is about ideas, not just process. Assemble accordingly.

The Step 2 checklist spells out all of the requirements necessary to put the right team together. It is designed to eliminate the Expert Loop, Overestimated Value, and Personal Prejudice, while incorporating Underestimated Value and Gut Instinct into the process.

STEP 2 CHECKLIST

- Our system improvement team leader has assembled a group of people that will represent a cross-section of ideas.

- Our team has a leader who champions our efforts, holds effective meetings, and is an effective change agent.

- We have invited people to our team that will challenge the status quo and seek improvement.

- Our team includes people who do the work in the system.

- Our team understands our customers.

- Everyone on our team offers ideas and alternatives (we encourage our talkers to listen and our listeners to talk).

- Our team meets face-to-face on a regular basis and is always properly prepared to contribute.

- Our team holds effective meetings with agendas, ground rules and documented action items for follow-up.

- Our team has a network of relationships who we rely on to bring us information and ideas (staff, crew, new employees, vendors, etc.).

- Our team avoids the "echo chamber": the same ideas over and over, just presented differently.

- Our team offers innovative and outside-the-box ideas.

- Our team holds themselves accountable to implementing changes, following through and tracking progress.

- Our team allows for disagreement, conflict, and challenge and builds trust by encouraging input and ideas that ultimately achieve system improvement.
- Our team learns from our failures.
- Our team celebrates success.
- Our team enjoys working together.

Each of these checklist items is important for the following reasons:

Our system improvement team leader has assembled a group of people that will represent a cross-section of ideas. As stated at the beginning of the chapter, it is important to actively seek out and engage participation from people who will represent a cross-section of ideas and perspectives. Quite often, the best ideas come from the most unexpected sources. Look for diversity in age, experience, education, background, industry, and so forth. The possibilities are endless, as are the potential ideas. As you assemble your list of potential team members, make sure to check for a majority of experts or those with overestimated value, as there is a likelihood they may dominate both the discussion and the idea flow. Challenge yourself to invite those from far outside your expected network. You may be surprised at their contributions.

It is the team leader's responsibility to ensure that the right mix of people have been assembled and to challenge automatic appointments by stakeholders or management. In turn, managers need to ensure that the team leader is also the most objective possible leader, that he is not so vested in the outcome of the system improvement that he may sway either the team or the results.

I have observed team leaders exhibit this lack of objectivity in past efforts. It can be both counterproductive and, in some cases, unethical. In one case, a senior floor manager at a large poultry processing plant was assigned as team leader to improve manufacturing productivity. Senior executives had assigned him the business goal of producing 15 percent more processed chicken parts. Competition had ramped up efforts and this client was losing its market share of some of the largest fast food corporations in the world. This assignment was not just about profit; it was about sustainability. In response to his assignment, the floor manager gathered a group of his employees to help with the project. He was told to work with us and incorporate our process improvement ideas into their efforts. After my team had performed an analysis, it was obvious that the floor was overstaffed, and that some of the functions being performed by hand could easily have been automated. As the team meetings progressed over the months, this team leader clearly had an alternate agenda. His dismissal of our input and ideas was blatant and clearly intentional.

It wasn't until many months later that we discovered he had presented his conclusions to the executive team, and that not one of our staff reduction or automation concepts had been suggested. Instead, he and his team recommended that the corporation buy a very large and expensive racking system, and essentially redirected the attention to a warehousing and logistics issue. We also discovered much later that this senior floor manager had ultimately been fired, once it was revealed that he had been receiving kickbacks in exchange for job security. By then, unfortunately, it was too late for my client, and the company ended up downsizing substantially and closing two out of its three product lines.

Our team has a leader who champions our efforts, holds effective meetings, and is an effective change agent.

As the leader or participant on a team dedicated to innovation and change (no matter the system), it is vital that the team has a leader who is not only passionate and committed, but who can also effectively and efficiently harness the energy of those around him, hold purposeful and productive meetings, and ultimately be the agent of change for that initiative. Without this leader, most change cannot be accomplished, as doing things differently can often cause such angst within an organization that any movement is stifled and new ideas wither on the vine.

I have witnessed some of the best ideas die off and become obsolete when not championed properly. I have also seen ideas that had great energy off the starting block only to die on the final straightaway. The leader of a system change effort must be its greatest champion, especially when enthusiasm wanes. It is critical for this same leader to hold meetings that do not waste others' time and that channel "idea energy" and not "meeting malaise."

If you find yourself holding brainstorming meetings that have zero energy or are simply fulfilling a meeting requirement, then these are not the right meetings. These meetings should be the ones that members look forward to, are energized by, and can't wait for the next one. The leader also needs to be the one who holds team members accountable to the rules and avoids the Expert Loop or danger of the Overestimated Value. He or she should actively gain participation, challenge the discussion, and capture the important outcomes of each meeting. Finding the right leader for your system improvement effort is absolutely vital. Without the right person championing the effort throughout all 9 Steps, the likelihood of success wanes.

We have invited people to our team who will challenge the status quo and seek improvement.

Not only do you want to invite a diverse crowd of participants to your team, but you want to include those who are willing to challenge the status quo. Keep in mind that these individuals may not always be viewed upon favorably (especially by management), but their opinions and observations can be valuable. Handled properly, their input can be essential to impacting the system in question. These same people may leave their organization when their ideas are met with resistance, to strike off on their own. Ultimately, these new ideas and people can become your own competition.

Most of us know who these people are: the squeaky wheels, those who eagerly and consistently like to challenge and push the envelope. Throughout history, these types of people are viewed upon by the majority with either disdain or dislike, or at a minimum, ambivalence. These are the people who bring attention to what is not right or what could be better. It is often the case that it is not until many years later that their message is finally heard or accepted, and only then are they perceived as visionary or a leader. Consider the example of Steve Jobs whose board of directors forced him out of his own company in the 1980s. Jobs was that squeaky wheel within his own organization, and upon his departure Apple almost became a footnote. It wasn't until his return and the innovation of the iPod, iPad, and iPhone that Apple made a comeback. Had Jobs taken these same ideas to another organization, Apple certainly would not have become the giant it is today.

It does not matter whether the people you invite to your system-improvement team effort only work within your system. In fact, bring the free-thinkers into the discussion. Ask the squeaky wheels what they think, what they would do. Often it is a completely unbiased and unvested perspective that can offer the freshest ideas.

Our team includes people who do the work in the system.

Ensure that the team assembled to provide suggestions for improvement includes those who actually *do* the work. This is important, as those with hands-on experience suffer most from inefficiencies.

One of the most interesting phenomena I have experienced around the implementation of the 9 Steps in various organizations is the highest interest at the lowest levels of the organization. On two separate occasions I have had the lowest-ranking person in the department come to me abuzz with ideas and excitement.

"Finally!" one junior accountant mentioned. "We have a way to fix things that we see every day." She was exasperated with an accounting process requiring three different people across three different departments multiple hours to complete one form, and all three people were submitting different versions of the same information to their supervisors. It was highly inefficient, and not something anyone not intimately familiar with the internal workings of the accounting department would ever have noticed.

She diligently followed the 9 Steps process, including performing an ROI analysis and the stated goal of saved labor dollars in each department. The fact that fixing this inefficiency would likely not save the organization large dollars in the grand scheme of things was inconsequential; it was the fact that she cared enough to want to fix it that mattered. This is the type of thinking you want to achieve throughout all levels (both vertically and horizontally) within your organization: a culture of employees that are interested in, and working toward, achieving their own system improvements no matter what the project, the process, or the job function is.

Involving this group of people in the brainstorming process and including them on system improvement teams can be very beneficial and eye-opening. They can serve as your sanity check, as they are most likely to know if the proposed solutions will work in the actual day-to-day experience of the job.

Our team understands our customers.

There are two types of customers relevant to your system: internal and external. Internal customers are those resources and functions within your business organization that will ultimately be impacted by any system improvement. It is important to recognize, involve, and document impacts to these customers. Likewise, it is essential that you monitor and track any impacts (both positive and negative) to your external customers, and ultimately whether these impacts may influence your organizational competitiveness in the market.

Always challenge your team to think in terms of end users and those who will ultimately utilize the system. System improvements mean nothing if they do not positively impact your business in a way that maintains or attracts new external customers and do not create inefficiencies or additional costs to your internal customers. At the end of the day, it should *always* be about money and the business goals of your organization.

Impacts to internal customers should not be underestimated. The interdependencies between internal and external customers should be seriously discussed and understood. In several system improvement projects in the past, I have observed how these interdependencies can ultimately influence the final optimal solution. In other words, although an improvement may positively impact your internal customer, it may not necessarily positively impact your external customer, and vice versa. What *is* important is the impact on your ultimate business goals. You must perform a cost-benefit analysis (Step 7) on whether the system improvement impacts your business goals (profit, safety, quality, etc.) and not the isolated impact on customers.

One client, a warehouse and distribution company for several of the largest coffee franchises in the world, wanted to find a way to improve its logistics efficiency. It was the company management's consensus that their warehousing process was inefficient and needed improvement in order to reduce both waste (perishables) and inventory in the warehouse. This client spent several hundred thousand dollars making improvements to its internal system (and internal customers in dispatch and distribution). Everyone within the organization was pleased and felt they had made great strides in improving efficiency. However, after implementation of their new and improved warehousing system, they found that actual delivery time to their external customers had increased and external customer satisfaction decreased. In fact, they began to lose some of their clients, the associated top-line revenue, and ultimately earnings. It was a harsh lesson in making sure to understand in entirety the impacts of any system improvements on all customers.

Everyone on our team offers ideas and alternatives (we encourage our talkers to listen and our listeners to talk).

Make sure to engage everyone on the team. Don't let the "talkers" dominate meetings with both their volume and ideas. Some of the best ideas come from the quietest participants.

My take on the interesting dynamic between talkers and listeners could be the subject of another book. I find personalities and the give-and-take between extroverts and introverts to be fascinating. There are many behavioral profiles and communication tests available that can be utilized to understand the styles of your team members, but in my opinion it boils down to simply watching how people behave in meetings. Your extroverts will talk and dominate. Your introverts will listen and choose their moments to participate. *An interesting side note: I observe this culturally, as well. For example, Americans tend to value those who are extroverted and dominate, while Canadians tend to value introverts who find consensus.*

Whatever the makeup of extroverts and introverts on your system improvement team, it is the team leader's responsibility to ensure that all participants get an opportunity to speak and present their input and ideas. Volume does not equal value. Find a balance.

Our team meets face-to-face on a regular basis and is always properly prepared to contribute.

Brainstorming and innovation are typically most effective when interpersonal dynamics are in play, and people are prepared to talk about the subject at hand. Remote online meetings simply do not generate the same energy or outcomes. People tend to communicate most effectively through tone and body language and the interplay of an active and spirited discussion.

One of the best brainstorming meetings I ever attended was held in Houston. It had the right makeup of participants (leaders, workers within the system, consultants outside the network, the young and inexperienced, and those more seasoned) and was held off-site from the business itself. Not only did the group visit several facilities with state-of-the-art equipment relevant to the system improvements, but members of the team came prepared with ideas and an agenda.

While we became mired a couple of times on the topic of ventilation (trust me, I never want to talk about that again), at the end of the three days we had selected the optimal solution and developed a plan to implement. We had worked through the ROI, we had followed the rules for brainstorming. This was a billion-dollar company. And a group of ten had inexorably altered the future of the company for the better.

Our team holds effective meetings with agendas, ground rules, and documented action items for follow-up.

In order for your team to remain engaged and committed to your efforts toward system improvements, it is critical that meetings are efficient, organized, and productive. Documented action items are not only important for the team as an accountability tool but also to the system improvement process in order to track progress and any change impacts. Ineffective and unproductive (and not very fun) meetings are one of the quickest ways to quash innovation and the desire to contribute. The rules of an effective meeting are simple:

Agenda: Prepare and distribute it ahead of time with assigned timeframes and topic owners. Make sure attendees know what to prepare and discuss. The leader is responsible for assembling and distributing.

Ground Rules: No phones or distractions, start on time and end early, take regular breaks, everyone participates, balanced and facilitated discussion, stay on topic.

Action Items: The leader is responsible for creating an Action Item list with the action, the owner, and the deadline, distributing the list after the meeting, and holding the team accountable to having completed their actions at the next meeting.

Simple, right? Not quite. One of the single largest complaints I hear from most employees (whether management or staff) regards inefficient meetings. So many meetings, so little accomplished. As leader, it is your job to avoid these problems and use your team's time wisely. It is a sign of respect and will set an excellent tone for participation in subsequent meetings.

Our team has a network of relationships that we rely on to bring us information and ideas (such as staff, crew, new employees, and vendors).

While not all members of the team need to attend every meeting, it is important to solicit input and ideas from a wide variety of relationships that impact the system under investigation. Not all individuals in your network need to attend all team meetings. They can be invited to attend as Subject Matter Experts (SMEs) on an as-needed basis.

The best way to manage this is to ensure that your agenda reflects not only what you will be discussing but who needs to be in attendance. It is perfectly acceptable to have different participants attend portions of meetings relevant to their expertise. Team leaders can assemble a "core" that is critical to all 9 Steps of the process and bring in SMEs during portions of each step. It is no different than effectively managing any project.

It is especially important if you are bringing in participants who "do the work" that you are not disrupting production or causing a ripple effect by their absence within their own department or process. Select your meeting times carefully and with thought, make sure to ask attendees how this meeting will impact their productivity, and ask if providing input via email will suffice if you need specific answers to specific questions. (This can be used for data or information-related topics, not for the brainstorming process.)

It is important to include consultants or outside sources of information as well during both the brainstorming (Step 6) and Implementation (Step 8) process. Other organizations can provide excellent benchmark data for new systems. I have been on some of these fact finding excursions, and meeting with people in industries outside your own is always eye-opening. I spent one day touring a Caterpillar facility, and as a result, we were able to completely rethink the material distribution process for my client who operates in an unrelated industry.

Our team avoids the "echo chamber": the same ideas over and over, just presented differently.

A primary reason for inviting a diverse group to the table is to avoid the same ideas being presented over and over. People tend to avoid meetings where they know new ideas are shut down and those with the highest seniority or loudest voice present their ideas continually.

By definition, an echo chamber is a closed system. Ideas in this type of environment are typically disallowed or censored to some degree. Employees learn to avoid both these types of meetings and the people who run them. When ideas or input are stifled, innovation cannot occur. A closed-loop system is not sustainable in business, as those things outside of your control will invariably impact your organization (such as the economy, force majeure, competitors, and new technology). Innovation is a vital component to growth and sustainability, and if your leadership operates within an echo chamber, your organization is highly likely to see decreased profit as a percentage of revenue.

Innovation is also cultural. Ask yourself if your organization supports an open culture, with new and fresh voices encouraged to bring their ideas to meetings and projects. Or, does your company simply recycle the ideas of the same few leaders who have been in key positions for many years? If you are struggling to grow both revenue and profit, the answer may be obvious.

Our team offers innovative and outside-the-box ideas.

The concept of outside-the-box thinking has been around for some time and has become almost cliché. However, bringing fresh concepts and ideas that are far outside the cultural or organizational norms can be both refreshing and invigorating.

One of my favorite stories involved a warehousing company in California. I had challenged management to start pushing down some of their goal meetings to lower and lower levels within the organization in order to gain buy-in and ownership of some of the business goals. One of the owners was both skeptical and a bit dismissive.

"Fine," he said. "Why don't we let the janitors hold a meeting?"

I thought this was a great idea. The maintenance folks I had met were tremendous. Hard-working, loyal and dedicated, these people were a committed and passionate group. Their de facto leader, Vanessa, a tall, single mother with long braids and a car that may or may not start in the morning, was thrilled when I told her of our plan. She immediately began campaigning her coworkers to participate, despite some misgivings on their part.

While these people toiled at sweeping, cleaning, mopping, and repairing three large warehouses and their affiliated offices and bathrooms, I noticed they demonstrated a culture of pride. Many of the job requirements were both demanding, occasionally disgusting, and often enlightening. (Note: Never, ever drink from a soda can without washing the top first. These cans sit in warehouses full of rodents, insects, and dirt for days.)

I had challenged this team to come up with ways to beat its own goals and be more productive. The staffers had set metrics around warehouse throughput and how their jobs could ultimately impact getting trucks into and out of the bays more efficiently. After several months of working together, this was a well-oiled maintenance machine. As often happens in these situations, the team wanted to do more. They had become a bit weary of trying to find ways to reduce janitorial costs and means to improve efficiency.

It was Vanessa who asked if they were allowed to offer ideas. I said, of course, anyone, anywhere within an organization can be innovative. She laughed and said that her team didn't believe the owners would listen even if they did. My response was simple: Do your math. Prove your idea. Over the next few months, I worked with Vanessa and her team to iron out a tremendous concept: She and her group had suggested that rather than throw away all of the pallets and waste, they set up a recycling center at the rear of the warehouse. Not only did the math prove out, but that recycling center became an earnings generator for the company. The owners were so impressed that they set up a profit sharing plan for the maintenance group. The end result for Vanessa? I can still see her ear-splitting grin the day I drove up and parked next to her brand new cherry-red car.

Our team holds themselves accountable to implementing changes, following through, and tracking progress.

It is critical as a team that you document and track not only your ideas but your decisions, in order to accurately measure your progress as well as any impacts to the business goals. It is also important that management see the fruits of your labor, and can adjust needed resources as required.

Documentation is a very important element of the 9 Steps process. The system improvement team needs to be able to track both its progress and any ideas offered. Sometimes one idea that may not gain traction at the front end may be the right answer later on. Additionally, adherence to the actual steps must be rigorous. The team leader cannot allow for shortcuts or any skipping of steps. The steps are designed to be sequential for a reason, as there are several loops designed to correct for errors. The forms (found at the end of each chapter in this book) are also designed to provide an accountability system so that both the system improvement leader and management are in sync with the team's progress and ideas, as well as which portions (and their affiliated costs) are to be implemented. This accountability is critical to both the team AND management.

Our team allows for disagreement, conflict, and challenge, and builds trust by encouraging input and ideas that ultimately achieve system improvement.

Some of the most productive meetings are the result of a healthy, challenging dialogue between team members, where ideas are gauged on relative merit, pros and cons are argued, and—ultimately—agreement and compromise are reached. Encouraging team members to disagree, rather than always reach consensus, is conducive to the process.

While in some organizational (and national) cultures conflict and dissent is discouraged, in the US this type of dialogue is generally acceptable. In my opinion it should be encouraged. Disagreement, (managed) conflict, and challenge should be reflective of passion and energy, not necessarily anger. Some of the most productive meetings I have attended include participants standing up and pacing the room, hands pulling with frustration through hair, vociferous and spirited discussion, jumping up and writing on a white board, and sometimes gut-wrenching laughter. It is this delicate balance of intensity and humor that can lead to some fantastic results.

I am not suggesting a free-for-all, nor am I suggesting that it be a yelling fest. What I am suggesting is that the energy of the group be harnessed and directed in ways that lead to ideas that matter, have relevance, and are reflective of the team's desire for improvement.

Our team learns from our failures.

As part of the documentation and tracking mechanism, it is important to understand those ideas or changes that were implemented but which failed. The team needs to learn from these outcomes, understand not just the what, but the why and how these outcomes could potentially influence other components of the system or even new ideas for change. It is also important to track all brainstorming ideas, as ideas that fail in one system improvement effort may be valuable to another.

In one situation, the team had brainstormed around the idea of an automation system for one portion of the manufacturing facility. At the end of the ROI analysis (Step 7) it was determined that the robotics would not pay off for that portion of the sub-assembly. However, several months later another portion of the facility was faced with the same challenge, and when the team was able to simply review the research and documentation provided by the previous sub-assembly system improvement team, it could make a decision quickly and efficiently to implement the automation into their portion of the process. The documentation (and failure) of the previous team saved months and months of time for this new team.

Our team celebrates success.

As with the failures, it is equally important to track and document those changes that were successful. But along with that, teams should spend some time actually celebrating success. One of the important emotional components of any continuous improvement effort is to sustain momentum within the employee base (morale, job satisfaction, retention, etc.) such that all contributing members of your system are motivated and committed to always thinking of new and better ways to impact the system. Reward and recognition are powerful tools that are often underutilized.

I have seen a wide spectrum of reward and recognition across many companies. In my opinion, the most important element is to know your employees. Don't assume you know what a celebration of success looks like, or what reward they will most appreciate. Ask them! Believe me, they will let you know. And when they succeed and you deliver, it is most definitely a win-win for all involved.

Our team enjoys working together.

Many of us have been on both winning and losing teams. There is a fundamental difference between the two. When you are on a team of either superstars who can't get along or a team of people not committed to or aligned with the goal, the effort is wasted. However, when the team enjoys each other's company, looks forward to meetings and feels that teamwork "mojo" that good teams perpetuate, magic can happen.

It is the team leader's responsibility to keep his finger on the pulse of this. It can be a difficult thing to actually track and measure, but a simple thing to feel. You either have the chemistry or you do not.

The team must speak up if the rules are not being followed, and the leader must watch the composition of members closely.

The LEGO Case Study According to Step 2:
Put the Right Team Together

One of the first things that Jorgen Knudstorp discovered in his corporate review was that current management really did not understand how far off track LEGO really was. It appeared that most employees and customers understood the problems, but these messages were not getting to the top. So Knudstorp assembled a team of experts including Jesper Ovesen, the new financial director, whose job it was to uncover the real financial situation. What he found was alarming: There were incorrect metrics measuring profitability and the company really did not know where they made money or lost money.

Knudstorp also conferred with Chris Zook of Bain and Company, and author of *Profit from the Core*, and found that LEGO's diversification situation was flawed. Knudstorp and Ovesen spent many hours brainstorming and discussing potential solutions with a diverse group of people, including those from outside their expected management network. As the leader of this team, Knudstorp championed the ongoing effort and clearly positioned himself as the team leader and change agent. In 2004, he was appointed CEO.

Step 2	THE RIGHT TEAM FORM			
	Name	**Position**	**Email**	**Phone**
Team Leader				
Team Member				
Team Member				
Team Member				
Team Member				
Team Member				
Team Member				

Management approval of team above: ▶ _____

Signature   Date

OUR TEAM

The team member list above fulfills the following: ✓

	✓
▶ Represents a cross-section of ideas	
▶ Is comprised of members who will challenge the status quo	
▶ There are members that do the actual work in the system	
▶ Our members understand our customers (internal and external)	
▶ Our members have networks to consult for additional information and ideas	

OUR MEETING GROUND RULES: ✓

	✓
▶ Our talkers listen, and our listeners talk	
▶ We meet face-to-face on a regular basis	
▶ Our team members are always prepared to contribute	
▶ We produce agendas, and documented action items	
▶ We avoid the echo chamber	
▶ We offer innovative and outside-the-box ideas	
▶ We hold ourselves accountable to our action items	
▶ We allow for disagreement, conflict and challenge, and build trust by encouraging input and ideas that ultimately achieve improvement.	
▶ We learn from our failures, celebrate success and enjoy working together	

Step 3:
Identify the Goal

"When defeat comes, accept it as a signal that your plans are not sound, rebuild those plans, and set sail once more toward your coveted goal."

NAPOLEON HILL
Think and Grow Rich

Identify a specific, measurable, achievable, and timely goal that will ensure that any improvements to the system will result in positive impacts to the business goals of the organization.

Aligning system improvements with the business goals of your organization is **critical** to making sound business decisions. Wasting time, money, personnel, and resources on ideas and proposed changes that will have little to no impact on the "business of your business" is pointless.

Even before you embark on any proposed changes to your system, you must first determine how any system improvements will impact the bottom-line business goals of your organization. While Step 1 (Identify the System That Needs Improvement) identifies the system improvement needed, as well as the initially *proposed* impacts on the organizational business goals, the form in Step 3 challenges the system improvement team to further refine both the scope of the proposed improvements, as well as the specific metrics devised to measure them.

There are several vital elements of every business—its Mission, Vision, and Values among them. Business goals are slightly different.

These are the elements of your business that are stripped away of language or message. In other words, at the end of the day if you do NOT reach these goals, you will no longer be in business. For example, making money MUST be a business goal. If your organization does not make money, then it is not ultimately sustainable. (I will not get into market valuations, principles of accounting, or nonprofits for the purposes of this book). I am simply talking about when top-line revenue less the cost of running your business less taxes at the end of the P&L leaves you some cash.

This is the first and foremost litmus test of any proposed change to any proposed system: if "x system" is improved, this improvement will result in increased margin/profit/earnings. Keep in mind that I am not speaking of revenue. Revenue is a different animal entirely. I have observed many businesses chasing revenue growth at the expense of profit. I've watched the delta between top-line revenue and profit (as a percentage of gross revenue) widen, as many of these companies continued under the illusion that they were *growing*. Indeed, that was not the case. If ever you find yourself selling more but making less, then you have fallen victim to this same delusion. As such, companies must watch their profit *as a percentage of revenue* and not simply as an absolute number, for this is truly where success is measured.

When assessing whether a system improvement or change to your business should be considered, it is important to take a step back and make sure you and your team understand the true business goals of your organization. I have used Profit, Safety, and Quality as examples in this chapter, but yours could be different. While profit must always be on the list, others could include Customer Satisfaction, Retention, Growth, Community Relations, and the like. In order to make sure you have selected the correct business goals, a quick and easy way to test whether you've selected the right goals is to ask yourself whether the business would lose money if this goal were compromised. Safety, for example, can be very costly for many industries. If you include safety as one of your business goals, then you must not sacrifice safety for increased production if in the end it erodes business profit. Likewise with quality; if you are able to produce widgets ten times faster, but at the end of the day quality decreases (and ultimately profit) then that system improvement was not successful. Everything must always be correlated to profit. Profit, profit, profit.

Profit is the only unit of measurement that truly reflects time, capital expenditures, people, equipment, and, ultimately, effort. It is the key metric that allows for growth and expansion, as well as organizational health. Profit allows for a Return on Investment (or Equity) for shareholders, bonuses for employees, and strategic choices for management. It is a mirror of your internal efficiencies and is highly reflective of how effectively senior management is paying attention. Profit can be achieved a multitude of ways: improved sales volume, increased market share, higher bid margin, improved internal efficiencies, reduced overhead, decreased losses, lower turnover, lean operations, reduced internal departments—the list is pretty long. I am continually amazed at how many businesses (regardless of their size) do not pay profit the proper respect that it deserves.

Both organizations and their management must understand not only the profit, but where it comes from. Are you making money due to market share? Are you making money because you were first to market? Do you understand your profit sources? Are you making money because you run a lean operation? Is 50 percent of your revenue generated from one source, but that source is only returning 5 percent, while another source may be generating a 12 percent return? Are you focused on the right things? Are your ideas for company-wide or internal system improvements targeting the largest contributors to profit? These are vital and important questions that must be at the forefront of the system improvement team's early discussions.

Consider the automotive industry. In the past, auto dealerships made money hand over fist but today they are only marginally profitable. While *revenue* may be generated from new car sales, most *profit* is generated by service and repair. Additionally, the profit margin on used cars is significantly higher than that of new cars. As a result, most dealerships have ramped up efforts to increase their used car fleets.

I worked with one automotive dealer off-and-on for over ten years. Because of the success of the used car portion of his dealerships, the owner made the strategic decision to invest in a new car dealership. He didn't do his homework well enough to understand that the amount of capital, time, energy, and resources required for the new car dealership would not return the proportionally same amount of profit. He thought that a system improvement (grow the brand) would generate more revenue, thus earnings. Despite increased unit sales, the end result was a dilution of his attention (as well as that of his staff), and a margin erosion that put his entire business in jeopardy. Luckily, he was (and is) a smart businessman and he figured it out in time to make adjustments.

Use the checklist on page 53 to ensure you are properly following Step 3.

STEP 3 CHECKLIST

- We understand the business goals of our organization (examples):
  - ○ Profit (must always be included)
  - ○ Quality (example)
  - ○ Safety (example)
- We have tied the goal of this system improvement to the business goals of our organization.
- This goal can be measured with specific metrics (Key Performance Indicators or KPIs) tied to the business goals of our organization.
- Once implemented, any changes to the system will result in positive impacts to the business goals of the organization, not just the system alone.
- We understand that the goal(s) we set for this system improvement may impact individual roles (positively and/or negatively), and we trust that the company will support our efforts.

Each are important for the following reasons:

We understand the business goals of our organization:
  - ○ *Profit*
  - ○ *Quality*
  - ○ *Safety*

It is important that at the onset of any efforts to improve your system, the team assigned to this effort is focused on making improvements that are aligned with the business goals of your organization. During the course of any discussions or brainstorming, ALWAYS go back to check if what you are proposing will ultimately impact your business goals in a positive manner. If the system change has little to no impact on one or more of the business goals, then it is not a valuable suggestion (later steps will address how to quantify and measure these impacts). Not only must the team assigned to system improvement know the business goals, they must also understand the interdependencies between them.

I had a client in the early 2000s who insisted the primary business goal of the organization was patient satisfaction. While admirable, I continued to push the management team to pay attention to less interesting metrics, and really hone in on profit and expenses. I worked very hard with the controller to develop a spreadsheet that accurately captured all of the operating expenses and revenue streams in order to quantitatively prove that the company was trending in the wrong direction. The CEO, however, insisted that the company was in prime condition since the patient satisfaction surveys improved month after month.

He was convinced that with these scores, word of mouth would spread that their services were superior to the competition (home health care). He truly believed that there was a direct correlation between these surveys and corporate success. Board meetings consisted of discussing copies of survey scores and patient letters. Nothing was said of the rising costs of nursing or that more and more companies were entering the industry, offering the same services at lower costs. It was clear from the financial spreadsheets that this company was not paying attention to increasing overhead and decreased market share. Management was NOT focused on the right business goals.

The end result was as expected. About a year later the company closed its doors. The message I want to stress in all of this is simple: there are many goals you can set for your customers, your employees, and your shareholders. But paramount to all of them (no matter how satisfying, contributory, well-meaning, interesting, or exciting they may be) is—you must make money.

We have tied the goal of this system improvement to the business goals of our organization.

The exercise of tying the goals or proposed system improvements to the goals of the organization are vital to any sustainable and viable continuous improvement effort. This should be a formal and ongoing part of the team's efforts, and the group should continuously "gut check" the outcomes of any improvement efforts against these same goals. Step 3 allows the system improvement team to vet the validity of the goal that was initially drafted in Step 1. Ultimately, this Step 1 goal should change and become much more refined and specific. An example of this transition might be:

Step 1 Goal: *Improve material throughput by 50 percent*

now becomes

Step 3 Goal:

- ○ *align material handling throughput capacity with fabrication facility*
- ○ *reduce welder manpower demands*
- ○ *reduce fabrication costs*
- ○ *meet or exceed project schedule*
- ○ *reduce rework*

As can be seen from this example, the original goal changed somewhat, which is perfectly acceptable as long as it remains in alignment with the business goals of your company. While in Step 1 you and your team realized that a system needed improvement and you established a preliminary goal, the purpose of Step 3 is to further refine this into a realistic and measurable result that does not put any of the overall business goals at odds with each other. In this example, improving material throughput is now broken into smaller, more measurable increments. The definition for throughput for every example is simply this: how your organization makes money. In this case, the concept of material throughput was assumed to be the system that ultimately generated the money. In fact, after the Step 3 analysis it was determined that throughput had to be aligned with capacity and operating expenses (welder manpower and rework). Additionally, those increments address one of the other business goals—quality (rework). Keep in mind that the definition of throughput put simply is "how your system generates money."

In the original goal of Step 1 above, the team identified the goal as "improve material throughput by 50 percent" which in and of itself is a good goal. It is clearly aligned with the business goal of profit and is easily measurable. However, upon further examination, the team assembled in Step 2 (the Right Team) determined that the Step 1 goal was not inclusive enough, and that they needed to be aware of the impacts on other portions of the system (material handling capacity and fabrication capacity), as well as quality (rework). It was decided early in the 9 Step process that one could not supersede the other (in this case increased throughput could not decrease quality). ALL of these incremental goals had to be met in order to achieve the ultimate goal of improved profit.

This goal can be measured with specific metrics (Key Performance Indicators or KPIs) tied to the business goals of our organization.

It is not sufficient to assume that any proposed changes to your system are tied to the business goals of the organization. In order to ensure that they do, you must tie metrics that are directly correlated to the business goals of your organization. For example, a simple performance metric is not enough—it must be a performance metric that can be tied directly to profit in dollars as well as any other business goals.

Keeping someone busy is not a correct metric if the **output** or **throughput** of that person is not directly contributing to profit. For example, a metric to measure system improvement would not necessarily come from a labor or cost report, but instead be tied directly to operations.

Examples might include: *% components not fabricated using robotics (throughput), or % on-time delivery (customer satisfaction), or # pieces received with incomplete information (quality).* Be careful of labor utilization as a metric. That can be a slippery slope since it is not a matter of busy people, but what busy people are producing that can actually generate profit dollars.

If you want to improve efficiency in a department that is not able to impact revenue or sales (a cost center instead) such as HR, IT, Administrative, Accounting, etc. you can certainly devise metrics that measure their ability to provide their function at the lowest cost. Reducing overhead is absolutely an effective way to positively impact profit and every employee in every department can, and should be, contributing to this effort.

I have worked with many support departments over the years and they are often surprised at how simple metrics can be. I have provided some samples below for these non-operational departments. *Note: It is critical that you have a UNIT OF MEASUREMENT within each metric (#, %, $, etc).* These are not meant to be all-inclusive, but do give an idea of how many possibilities exist. Keep in mind that each of these need to have a time stamp of either per week, per month or per year and should be tracked in the following categories:

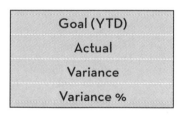

| Goal (YTD) |
| Actual |
| Variance |
| Variance % |

Human Resources

- # voluntary turnover
- # involuntary turnover
- % retention
- % manager attrition

- # open positions
- # average days to hire position
- # interns hired/employment
- # recruits
- # recruits interviewed/# hired
  (provides a process effectiveness ratio)
- # training hours/employee
- # employee complaints
- # days to HR issue resolution
- # days labor disputes outstanding
- $ workers compensation claims
- $ insurance

Accounting

- # average day sales outstanding
- % accounts 30/60/90 days past due
- $ Accounts Payable
- $ Accounts Receivable
- # paycheck errors
- # days end of month cost report available to
  management
- # accuracy errors (per report)
- # cost reports/accounting FTE
- Financial
- $ Revenue by location/market/client
- $ Cost of Goods Sold
- $ Operating Expense by Department
- $ Operating expense/FTE
- $ Expenses (as % of revenue in descending order)
- $ Total Expenses

- ○ $ Net income
- ○ $ Net Income as % of revenue
- ○ $ Revenue per FTE
- ○ $ Margin per FTE
- ○ $ EBITDA
- ○ % Return on Investment
- ○ % Return on Equity
- ○ $ Revenue/Salaried Man Year
- ○ Net Gain/Salaried MY
- ○ Net Gain/Share

Safety

- ○ # Meetings
- ○ % Sign Off
- ○ # First Aids
- ○ # Incidents
- ○ # Accidents
- ○ # Recordables
- ○ # Recordables/FTE
- ○ $ Safety Training
- ○ % FTE Safety Trained
- ○ # Incidents/Client

Quality

- ○ # Quality Incident Reports
- ○ $ Rework/Client
- ○ $ Rework/Part
- ○ $ Rework/linear foot
- ○ # Weld repairs/inch
- ○ # customer returns/location

○ % customer complaints/product

○ # Errors/batch

○ % Rejection/product/batch/line

For operations, there are far too many to list here, but I will continue to provide examples within each step. Note that operations metrics should be aligned as much as possible with the concept of *throughput*—something we will discuss in entirety in Step 5: Identify Bottlenecks within the System.

Once implemented, any changes to the system will result in positive impacts to the business goals of the organization, not just the system alone.

Another important element of measuring and understanding both the goal of your system change, as well as the business goals of the organization, is whether or not the changes to your system will *ultimately* impact the business goals of the larger organization, and not just within the system itself.

For example, producing more welds is not a positive change unless it positively impacts the delivery of the project to the client. If, conversely, producing more welds results in a backload of work-in-progress, and negatively impacts the throughput of your overall system, then more welds has a negative impact to your system.

It is acceptable to have this understanding at this point without a complete analysis. Step 5 will provide an in-depth analysis of whether or not you are looking at the business as a whole or if your desire for improvements to your own system has clouded your acceptance of potential negative impacts on the overarching business goals of your organization. At this stage, simply acknowledging that it may happen is sufficient. There are additional checks and balances in later steps to ensure that you have stayed within the boundaries of your system improvement and not impinged upon other areas, while ultimately negatively impacting business goals.

STEP 3—IN THE REAL WORLD

For Client A many of the factors that led to the losses in fabrication productivity were discussed during the 2013 and 2014 business planning cycles. Potential contributors to losses included: increased safety requirements, lack of training, unqualified personnel, communication breakdowns, increasingly complex projects, lack of automation, and an ongoing lack of accountability. Unit rates were continuing to creep up on an annual basis, and no single system of accountability was in place to curb these costs. Management knew that trying to tackle every single contributing factor to unit rate increases would only lead to a dilution of effort with no real results. Instead, it focused on a single, unified goal—"reduce production unit rates by 40 percent." And to focus this goal on the business goal of making money, those cost codes that were contributing to the largest losses were focused on first. This message was reinforced throughout 2014 and 2015 operational meetings, with plenty of public discussion throughout the company around the importance of achieving this goal.

The teams assigned to achieving this ambitious goal understood that in doing so, they may indeed change some of Client A's internal processes, as well as perhaps even their own individual roles and responsibilities. In alignment with Step 2, this acknowledgment was an important early element of their success.

We understand that the goal(s) we set for this system improvement may impact individual roles (positively and/or negatively), and we trust that the company will support our efforts.

One very important element of introducing any change within a system is the impact of that change on those that actually perform the work. In some cases, successful changes may result in the individual's efforts being negatively impacted, while the impact to the system as a whole is positive. *Note: an example of a negative impact could mean loss of that position (negative for that person but positive for the business goals), change in that position's function or duties, or reduced availability of hours for that employee.*

It is important that the team implementing the changes, the management approving the changes, and the organization that is accepting these changes, works in concert to communicate these impacts clearly, and promotes a culture of trust and transparency that allows for the individual to move freely within the system (with the understanding that roles and responsibilities my change.)

This can be exceptionally tricky within large organizations that have a well-established culture. Many employees (especially tenured ones) can be highly resistant to any changes, and may actually work counter to your desire to improve any parts within their own systems. I have witnessed this phenomena many times: where employees actively attempt to sabotage improvement efforts in order to protect their individual interests. I have found that if the team understands this risk early on and everyone works together, that the likelihood of this decreases.

Typically, teams and the organizations will work together to place employees into new roles or other functions. It is rarely the case that individuals or teams are unilaterally terminated.

The LEGO Case Study According to Step 3:
Identify the Goal

In Ashcroft's analysis, he identifies multiple issues within LEGO that were likely contributing to any number of problems: management was out of touch with major customers, new products were competing for space on shelves already overstocked, too many newly introduced products, and distracting theme parks, to name a few. Yet, at the very beginning it was the LEGO team led by Knudstorp that identified the single goal that it needed to focus on: manage the business for *cash* rather than sales growth. And this meant making some tough decisions and implementing some serious changes. In order to identify this goal, Knudstorp clearly needed to understand the business goals of his organization, create clear metrics to measure progress towards those goals, and ultimately, any proposed changes to his system (organization) could quite possibly change his or anyone's titles or levels of authority.

For example, one area of disconnect identified in Ashcroft's case study was a lack of profitable innovation—where sales had increased, but profitability had shrunk. Had LEGO only focused on this one element within its overall system (organizational) improvement, it may have missed improving the overall business goal of *organizational* profitability. In other words, even if LEGO had introduced profitable products, it still may not have overcome organizational losses within other divisions/functions of the company. As such, it is critical to clearly understand the goal of your system improvement and tie it directly to the business goals of your organization.

Step 3	GOAL FORM

We commit, both individually and as a team, to system improvement goals that positively impact our organization, with the understanding that it may simultaneously impact individuals/departments positively or negatively. We trust that the company will support both the decisions and the individuals.

Our system improves these business goals (may be one or more):

Business goals of our organization	
Profit:	▶
	▶
Safety:	▶
	▶
Quality:	▶
	▶

Specific Key Performance Indicators tied to business goals (may be one or more):

Profit/Productivity KPI	▶
	▶
Safety KPI	▶
	▶
Quality KPI	▶
	▶

Management Approval: ▶

Signature   Date

Step 4:
Observe the System

"Nothing has such power to broaden the mind as the
ability to investigate systematically and truly
all that comes under thy observation in life."

—MARCUS AURELIUS
Meditations Book III

*Utilize the correct analysis tools appropriate to your system, include
and listen to input from those involved, observe objectively, document,
and present findings.*

Once you have clarified the parameters of your system, identified
the goals of your improvements, and tied those directly to the business
goals of your organization, you are now ready to begin observation of your system. It may sound as if it's a simple step, but much can
be lost during the course of this step by either lack of proper documentation, or otherwise "filtering" system observations due to personal or organizational bias.

Observation by definition is the front-end process of information
gathering. By its very nature it is intended to be completely objective
and unbiased. For the 9 steps to work, any evidence or data collected
must follow the same process as any scientific method. In other
words, the team must utilize the formal scientific method of forming
questions or hypotheses (in this case the hypothesis can simply be "we
are able to improve this system") and then acquiring the knowledge

that will either support or disprove that the system can be improved by changing it. This is exactly where the collection of the empirical data becomes important. This empirical research involves collecting measurements, information, or data through direct observation of the system. Quantitative research can be used to collect numerical data (time studies, etc.). In some cases, it may be important to also use qualitative methods (visual observations of behaviors).

The objectivity of this information is essential to this step. It may be prudent, in some cases, to use individuals who have no knowledge of the desired system improvements in order to remove any unintentional or subliminal bias. I have seen this happen on many occasions; well-meaning individuals want something to change so badly that they falsely report information.

This can happen either during the observation phase of the original system or during the post-change analysis. Either way, it skews the results and discredits the 9 step process. In one instance I was working with a small start-up company founded by a very intelligent entrepreneur. He had developed an electronic system for an automotive application that had tremendous potential. As you might imagine, no one wanted this thing to work more than the group of scientists and engineers developing it. Unfortunately, one research scientist had become so zealous about the need for the technology that he allowed his personal bias and desire for success to cloud his objective observations and use of the scientific method. It wasn't until much later that both investors and board members alike discovered that he had fudged the numbers.

When asked why he did it, he replied, "I figured I could redesign it in time for the numbers to catch up."

The fallout from that mistake delayed development and funding to the point that the competition eventually caught up and this company could no longer be first to market. So no matter your personal desires or objectives, if you are charged with observing a system, report what you actually observe, not what you *think* you observed, not what you *wish* you observed, but only what actually occurred.

Management of the observation process and the people involved is important. The system improvement team leader needs to choose his/her observers carefully. Checks and balances must occur along the way to ensure data reliability. It is also very important to make sure that your team understands whether system observation should occur with the workers within the system either "in the know" or "not in the know." If the team feels behaviors will change when people are being observed, then perhaps a covert approach should be used. If this is not of concern, then make sure that the workers know that they are being observed and why. It is in the team's best interest to involve the workers in ongoing discussions about system improvements since they are most likely to know exactly where opportunities for improvement exist.

Step 4 is designed to provide the tools necessary to accomplish all of the above. Both the checklist and the form have key accountability and sign-off functions to improve the reliability of the results.

STEP 4 CHECKLIST

- We are observing only the system identified in Step 1.
- We have engaged all relevant stakeholders in our observations.
- We have observed and communicated with all stakeholders in our system.
- We used _____ (name a specific analysis tool) to observe our system.
- We have taken photos and videos of our observations.
- We have created a visual representation or simulation of our observations.
- We have documented our observations.

- We have not biased our observations; they are objective and analytical.
- We have organized and filed our observations in a manner that can be easily identified, accessed, and duplicated by others.
- We have created a summary presentation of our observations that tie to our business goals.
- We have presented our findings to the right audience for feedback.
  - The individuals involved in the system we observed
  - The appropriate decision-makers
  - All stakeholders
- Our system improvement team leader has approved our observation plan prior to beginning any system observations.

The Step 4 checklist is designed to ensure proper observation of your system.

Each of these steps is important for the following reasons:

We are observing only the system identified in Step 1.

In Step 1, your team identified a system that produces work inefficiently and determined that if it were improved, it would positively impact the business goals of the organization. When beginning the observational phase, it is important to clearly delineate the start and end points of your system as defined in Step 1, as well as make sure you are only observing the system within those parameters. System boundaries are key to understanding how the actual changes are impacting the system that has been defined. Observations outside of your system boundaries will muddy the waters and make the before and after system comparisons difficult to ascertain.

STEP 4—IN THE REAL WORLD

In the case of Client A, the timing of current projects and new customers helped to force the process of system improvement. The newest project was well underway, and this enabled the team to observe the ongoing fabrication process. Rather than rely solely upon their own observations, the team elected to bring in an independent group to perform a modified Kaizen. This was a new and different way of doing things for Client A, but they knew the way they had been trying to fix things was just not working any longer. In addition to the analysis tool, the team supplemented those observations with a team of young, fresh-eyed engineers to observe the process with the idea that they would not have much historical bias. Observations were grouped into Safety, Quality, and Productivity, documented and prioritized accordingly.

The group performed some modeling and observed the work plans step-by-step (material handling, cranes, fitting, welding, etc.). These observations were captured in a spreadsheet characterized by High, Medium and Low observed impacts to the system. Input was gathered from craft performing the work and the data was checked and re-checked for any observational bias. Photos, videos, and notes were captured and documented in a Field Operations Report that could be used for future analyses and observation.

It can be very tempting to throw everything and the kitchen sink into early discussions about improvements. Many conversations devolve quickly when this starts to happen. I've coined this the "if we" phase. In other words, Jim offers "well, if we fix A then B" and Sherry adds "yes, if we include C, then A is even better," while Andy offers that in reality they should be including X. Conversations become long conceptual rants with little to no structure. While these can be fun, ultimately they are not productive and should be saved for the brainstorming portion of the 9 steps (Step 6). It is important for the individuals who have been charged with the observation stage to be made fully aware of the system parameters going in. It can be tempting for them to go wildly off-track.

Case in point: We had assigned a team of smart, energetic, innovative (young) engineers to go into the system identified in Step 1 at a large manufacturing facility. They were charged with observing and reporting back their unbiased observations of the robotics cell - a section of the shop with large robotic arms that moved components around into preset measurements for laser cutting. The arms eliminated the need to manually maneuver by hand and re-measure after every setting. For some reason, material in that section of the shop was building up prior to the robotics cell (the true definition of a "bottleneck"). The engineers were given three weeks to complete their observations, return to the system improvement team, and report the methodology and tools they used and what they observed.

I distinctly remember sitting in the meeting with the system improvement team eagerly awaiting the report. We had spent many months diligently identifying the system, picking the right team, assigning system boundaries, and ensuring we were using the right observation tools. Quite a bit of time and resources had been expended on this effort, and a lot was riding on this meeting. The team of eight or so people sitting around the table was very interested to learn what they had found.

We began the process of going through the Step 4 form (at the end of this chapter) and were about halfway through the meeting when one of the young engineers hopped up and said he wanted to give a PowerPoint presentation of his findings. He got through about fifteen minutes of his presentation before the boss shut him down. It seems the young engineer, while observing the robotics system, had decided that what was really a much more important (and interesting) system improvement was to reduce heat and energy waste throughout the facility (something he observed while in the cell, but obviously not within the system boundaries). While it was an interesting concept, it did not meet the criteria of Step 4 whatsoever, and ultimately that sidebar cost the system improvement effort almost two months—and that engineer his position on the system improvement team.

Note: I am happy to report that the young engineer rebounded mightily and started his own firm. He has since built a potentially industry-changing technology around his ideas. So this story has a bit of a twist—but for the purposes of the 9 Steps: stick within your boundaries. But for overall system improvements, keep those big brain, game-changer ideas as part of another discussion. If you decide that the big brain idea will make you more money in the end, by all means follow that path. In this case, this engineer's big brain idea would likely not have gotten much traction within that particular company since it did not have the revenue potential that it would in other industries, so his decision to go it alone was correct. His departure was also the appropriate business decision for the company.

We have engaged all relevant stakeholders in our observations.

During system observations, it is important to engage all relevant stakeholders, that is, anyone impacted by potential system changes as well as those actually doing the work within the system, in your observations. This will alleviate any suspicion or concerns, which in turn could lead to false behaviors and performance within the system. It may also be that during this stage that new and innovative ways of performing within the system may be offered as a result of being observed. Plan your observation times carefully. Make sure to observe during both peak and non-peak hours. Understand ahead of time what you must observe and what the individual functions of those involved should be. Some very important observations may be that key operators within the system are performing functions either outside the scope of their duties, or performing functions that are counter to productivity within their system. Understanding what these roles and responsibilities should be, as opposed to what they *actually* are, prior to the actual observation, is important so that observers realize that these functions are either (a) incorrect or (b) could be improved.

Also keep in mind that stakeholders can be non-operators *outside* the system (their operations are conducted separate and apart from yours), but they have input *inside* the system boundaries. For example, if part of your system involves an outside department or vendor that supplies information, parts, equipment, resources or anything else relevant to your system, and their function impacts your system, then, they too should be part of the discussion.

I have seen many large projects suffer from outside department, vendor, and subcontractor mismanagement. While my concept of mismanagement may be different from others, I believe that many businesses simply do not fully understand either the cost or time impact that their internal departments, outside vendors, and subcontractors have on their projects. Many assume that because a job is assigned, a contract is signed, and a delivery date is set, that they can continue along their way with little or no understanding of the operations of these other departments or outside firms. Especially in large operations this can be wildly inaccurate and extremely costly. Understanding *exactly* how suppliers and vendors impact your internal system is critical to truly understanding your overall system. Whether it is something as simple as printer ink or as vast as a multi-million dollar generator, the impact to your bottom-line can be enormous. I have seen both cripple a project.

In one case, the printer ink problem caused a bid to be late and cost a large firm the opportunity to win an enormous project. (In those days you had to submit multiple printed copies; electronic only just would not do.) Unfortunately, the proposal staff assumed that the cabinet was full of cartridges. The admin assumed that the proposal staff would ask her when they were running low. Neither thought to check whether they would be available at crunch time. In this example I am sure that those who assembled the information for the bid never would have assumed that another department could impact their ability to meet the schedule (and win the job). That was an expensive lesson.

In the case of the multimillion dollar piece of equipment (an enormous turbine generator), since it was on the schedule as a milestone, everyone assumed that the procurement department had it handled. It was the single largest piece of equipment in the assembly and its installation was on the critical path. Ample time was spent discussing the generator's production, sub-assembly, and delivery date by the supplier. However, what the project team missed was that this supplier had an (easily researchable) history of missing delivery dates by months and sometimes years. At the outset this equipment manufacturer had steadfastly assured everyone in the procurement department that all dates would be met and no issues were forthcoming. However, when it was time for the piece of equipment to be loaded onto the barge for its journey across the ocean, suddenly days started slipping. As days turned into weeks, frantic phone calls did nothing to hasten the delivery. Several months went by and other project milestones were missed. The project manager nearly lost his mind. Here he was, after years of hard work, in the final stages of the project watching both his schedule and budget slip through his fingers with one supplier. It was heart-wrenching and stressful for everyone involved. The project manager and his boss even flew overseas to the supplier to try to move things along, but to no avail. In the end, this supplier single-handedly delayed the project by eight months and millions upon millions of dollars.

So know not only your system, but all key stakeholders and relevant parties affecting your system. This knowledge can make a tremendous difference in outcomes.

We have observed and communicated with all stakeholders in our system.

As I described above, it is important that you not only share with your stakeholders what you are observing, but why you are observing it. Eliminate potential fear and resistance by encouraging their input and solutions, instead of increasing paranoia and fear that system changes may result in job obsolescence.

In the example of the robotics cell, the operators of the robotic arms and laser systems knew they were going to be observed. At first, the supervisor approached the improvement team leader with trepidation: he was worried that this might mean his guys would lose their jobs. When he learned that the team was not there to condemn or replace anyone, but rather to solve a problem, he offered both his and his team's input, and the situation changed dramatically. The operators became quite engaged and actually joined several of the meetings. Their insight and ideas proved instrumental to providing answers to the system issues. In fact, in the second round of observations, the supervisor suggested several key observations that proved very valuable to the ongoing improvement efforts. Without his input, it is unlikely the observation team would have discovered this on their own.

We used _____ (name a specific analysis tool) to observe our system.

This is likely the most difficult and complex portion of the 9 Steps process—and typically where most organizations fail. They are either unwilling or unable to allocate the time and resources to this effort. I must admit I spend an inordinate amount of time simply convincing organizations of the need to perform this analysis. Most companies prefer to rely on their own internal information and overly simple observations. Many assume that this approach will suffice. If it did, then you are already making the most amount of money you can, your organization is safe and producing the best quality product possible. So you do not need these 9 Steps.

In order to make this as understandable and applicable as possible a quick series of definitions and examples of the tools available is provided. This list is not at all comprehensive. There are many tools available. Appendix C supplements this section with further examples of types of tools that can be utilized to observe your system. We will briefly review the most common tools: Fishbone Diagram, Kaizen, DCMA, Root Cause Analyses (RCA), Job Hazard Analyses (JHA) and others, all of which can be used to observe current systems. No matter what tools you use, the purpose remains the same: to properly, methodically, analytically and systemically observe and document your system in a way that can be reproduced and analyzed quantitatively and objectively by others.

The reason for using analytical tools is simple: the observer *must* remove any personal or organizational bias from the results; otherwise the results are false. If your system is a business or process system (non-production or operations) the methodology remains of the same, while the system specifics may differ. Do not assume you can skip this step if you work within an internal department and your "operations" are not directly tied to a project or operations process.

The following provides a brief overview of each of these types of observational systems. *Warning: this may be a boring section, but it is absolutely necessary in order to follow the 9 Steps accurately and thoroughly.* This analysis and understanding of your business processes is key to making improvements. This section is in no way meant to replace researching or utilizing experts in these areas to assist in the analysis efforts. In fact, I highly recommend hiring people who are good at this to objectively observe and provide recommendations to your systems, especially if they are complex. This section is, however, meant to provide you with an overview of the value and application of each of these tools, as well as provide guidelines for how they can be used within your organization. It does not matter what type of business you operate: hospital, banking, manufacturing, accounting, engineering, technology, research—the list is endless. Each of these tools can be applied to you in some form or another. It is simply a matter of application and effort.

The Fishbone Diagram

Perhaps the simplest tool to use is the fishbone diagram, also called a cause-and-effect diagram or Ishikawa diagram. This tool is a visualization tool for categorizing the potential causes of a problem in order to identify its root causes. This tool is especially useful in departments such as human resources, IT, accounting, and others where a more complicated analysis tool may not be necessary. The design of the diagram looks much like a skeleton of a fish. Fishbone diagrams are typically worked right to left, with each large "bone" of the fish branching out to include smaller bones containing more and more of the details.

The fishbone is credited to Dr. Kaoru Ishikawa, a Japanese quality control expert who invented the fishbone diagram to help employees avoid solutions that merely address the symptoms of a much larger problem. Fishbones are often applied when:

○ You need to study a problem or issue to determine its root cause

○ You want to examine all possible reasons why a process is flawed or has become a bottleneck in your system and is not producing the desired results consistently

A fishbone diagram can be very useful in brainstorming sessions and enables focused conversations. After the group has brainstormed all the possible causes for a problem, the leader or facilitator helps the group to rate the potential causes according to their level of importance. Once completed, attendees can diagram a hierarchy.

Note: Fishbone diagrams are also used in the "analyze" phase of Six Sigma's DMAIC (define, measure, analyze, improve, control) approach to problem solving that will be explained further in the chapter.

So how is a fishbone diagram constructed? The following provides a brief overview:

1. Draw the basic fishbone diagram.

2. Write the problem or issue to be studied at the "head of the fish" on the right.

3. For each "bone" of the "fish," provide a category of the problem area:

   ○ The 4 M's: Methods, Machines, Materials, Manpower

   ○ The 4 P's: Place, Procedure, People, Policies

   ○ The 4 S's: Surroundings, Suppliers, Systems, Skills

4. Use brainstorming to capture the issues within each category that may be affecting the system or the effect being studied. The team should ask questions like "what are the machine issues affecting?" or "which materials are we consistently missing?" Write these on the "bones" stemming from the category bone.

5. Repeat this procedure with each factor under each category to produce sub-factors. Continue asking, "Why is this happening?"

6. Continue until you no longer get useful or new information.

7. Analyze the results after team members agree that an adequate amount of detail has been provided under each major category. Those items that appear in more than one category become the most likely causes.

8. These most likely causes should then be ranked by the team to determine the priority from the most probable cause to the least probable cause.

The example in figure 4-1 illustrates a fishbone diagram that might identify all the possible reasons a website went down in order to discover the root cause. Figure 4-2 gives a more detailed example of constructing a fishbone diagram.

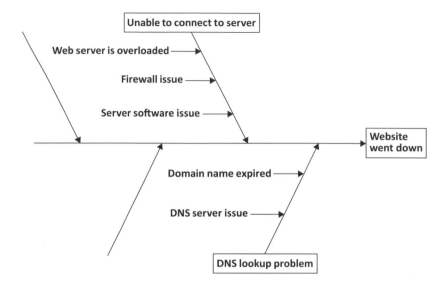

Figure 4-1 *Example of a simple fishbone diagram*

Root Cause Analysis (RCA)

RCA is a method of problem solving used to identify the root causes of faults or problems. RCA is applied to methodically identify and correct the root causes of events rather than to simply address the symptomatic result. The correction of root causes is meant to prevent the problem or issue from recurring.

RCA is not one single, sharply defined methodology. Instead, RCA comprises many different tools, processes, and philosophies. Several broadly defined approaches or "schools" can be identified by their basic approach or field of origin: safety-based, production-based, assembly-based, process-based, failure-based, and systems-based. RCA developed in the 1950s as a formal study by the National Aeronautics and Space Administration (NASA). One NASA-based example might include whether an aircraft accident occurred as a result of adverse weather conditions augmented by pressure to leave on time. This failure to observe weather precautions could indicate a management or training problem as well as a lack of appropriate work practices.

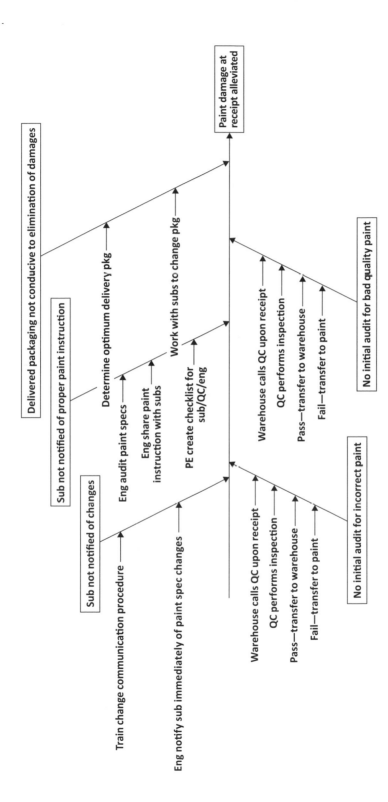

Figure 4-2 Example of a more detailed fishbone diagram

Another example could include an investigation into a machine that stopped working. All indications are that it overloaded and the fuse blew. Observations of this system conclude that the machine overloaded because it had a bearing that wasn't being sufficiently lubricated. The team investigates further to find that the automatic lubrication mechanism had an insufficient pumping mechanism that contributed to the lack of lubrication. Investigation of the pump shows that it has a worn shaft. Review of the shaft indicates that there is not an adequate mechanism to prevent scrap metal from entering the pump. As a result, the scrap metal damaged the pump. The root cause of the problem is therefore that metal scrap can contaminate the lubrication system. Fixing this problem should prevent recurrence. If the investigation concluded that replacing the fuse, the bearing, or the lubrication pump would have only solved the problem in the short term and the machine problem would likely have recurred.

RCA is an iterative process and considered a tool of continuous improvement.

- Safety-based RCA arose from the fields of accident analysis and occupational safety and health.

- Production-based RCA has roots in the field of quality control for industrial manufacturing.

- Process-based RCA, a follow-on to production-based RCA, broadens the scope of RCA to include business processes.

- Failure-based RCA originates in the practice of failure analysis as employed in engineering and maintenance.

- Systems-based RCA has emerged as an amalgam of the preceding schools, incorporating elements from other fields such as change management, risk management, and systems analysis.

Despite these somewhat divergent approaches among the various schools, all share some common principles. Several general RCA processes include:

1. The primary aim of root cause analysis is to identify the factors that resulted in the nature, the magnitude, the location, and the timing of the harmful outcomes (consequences) of one or more past events; to determine what behaviors, actions, inactions, or conditions need to be changed; to prevent the recurrence of similar harmful outcomes; and to identify lessons that may promote the achievement of better consequences. Success is defined as the near-certain prevention of recurrence.

2. In order to be effective, root cause analysis must be performed systematically as part of Step 4 with conclusions and root causes that are identified, documented, and filed appropriately. The system improvement team should lead this effort.

3. Since there are often more than one root cause for an event or a problem, the team must remain diligent in uncovering each and every one.

4. The purpose of identifying all solutions to a problem is to prevent recurrence at the lowest cost and in the simplest way. If there are alternatives that are equally effective, then the simplest or lowest cost approach is preferred. This is in alignment with the business goal of profit.

5. The root causes identified will depend on the way in which the problem or event is defined. As noted in Step 3, the identification of the goal statement is critical.

6. RCA should establish a sequence of events or timeline for understanding the relationships between contributory (causal) factors, root cause(s) and the defined problem or event to be prevented. It is always a good idea to create a visual aid to follow this sequence.

Define   Measure   Analyze   Improve   Control

Figure 4-3 *The five improvement steps of DMAIC*

DMAIC

DMAIC is an acronym for *Define, Measure, Analyze, Improve*, and *Control*. This analysis method refers to a data-driven improvement cycle used for improving, optimizing, and stabilizing business processes and designs. This is a common tool used to get at the heart of many business issues and inefficiencies. The DMAIC improvement cycle is the core tool used to drive Six Sigma projects (but is not exclusive to Six Sigma).

DMAIC is an abbreviation of the five improvement steps it comprises: Define, Measure, Analyze, Improve, and Control. All of the DMAIC process steps are required and always proceed in the given order.

Define

The purpose of this step is to clearly articulate the business problem, goal, potential resources, project scope and high-level project timeline. The system improvement team would follow these steps in order and define the following:

- A problem
- The customer(s)
- Voice of the customer (VOC) and Critical to Quality (CTQs)—what are the critical process outputs?
- The target process subject to DMAIC and other related business processes

○ Project targets or goal statement

○ Project boundaries or scope

○ The goal of this effort (often referred to as the project charter)

Measure

This step objectively establishes current baselines as the basis for improvement. This is a data collection step only used to establish process performance baselines. The idea here is to create tangible metrics that can be used to compare to any future improvements. The system improvement team decides on what should be measured and how to measure it. It is usual for teams to invest a great deal of effort into assessing the suitability of the proposed measurement systems. Good data is at the heart of the DMAIC process:

○ Identify the gap between current and required performance.

○ Collect data to create a process performance capability baseline for the project metric.

○ Assess the measurement system for adequate accuracy and precision.

○ Establish a high level process flow baseline. Additional detail can be filled in later. Tools like Viseo can be helpful for this.

Analyze

The analyze step identifies, validates, and selects root causes for elimination. A large number of potential root causes of the project problem are identified utilizing a root cause analysis (such as the fishbone diagram above). The top few potential root causes are selected using the system improvement team voting or other consensus tool for further validation. A data collection plan is created and data are collected to establish the relative contribution of each of the root causes to the project metric.

This process is repeated until "valid" root causes can be identified. Within Six Sigma, often complex analysis tools are used. However, it is acceptable to use basic tools if these are appropriate. To validate root causes:

- List and prioritize potential causes of the problem.
- Prioritize the root causes (key process inputs) to pursue in the Improve step.
- Identify how the process inputs affect the process outputs. Data should be analyzed to understand the magnitude of contribution of each root cause to each project metric. Statistical tests using p-values accompanied by Histograms, Pareto charts, and line plots are often used to do this.
- Detailed process maps can be created to help pinpoint where in the process the root causes reside, and what might be contributing to the occurrence.

Improve

The purpose of this step is to identify, test and implement a solution to the problem; in part or in whole. We will not spend an inordinate amount of time on this step as it is covered in Steps 6 through 9 of the 9 Steps process.

Control

The purpose of this step is to sustain the gains and monitor the improvements to ensure continued and sustainable success. The team must create a control plan and update all documents, business process and training records as required.

A control chart can be useful during the Control stage to assess the stability of the improvements over time by serving as a guide for continuous monitoring and a response plan for each of the measures being monitored in case the process becomes unstable. This can be very important as oftentimes focus is removed from this system improvement and on to others.

Kaizen

Kaizen is a lean manufacturing tool that drives continuous improvement in any business process. Kaizen is a more manufacturing specific tool (and somewhat more complex) but can also be applied to any business process even if it does not involve manufacturing.

Kaizen was first developed during the effort to rebuild Japan after World War II. In that effort, several US business consultants collaborated with Japanese companies to improve manufacturing techniques. That collaboration resulted in the development of several new management techniques, one of which was Kaizen. Kaizen comes from two Japanese words: Kai (improvement) and Zen (good). Upon Toyota's success using Kaizen, it became widely known as "continuous improvement."

Kaizen works by reducing waste and eliminating work processes that are overly difficult. It is a tool used to increase overall business efficiency, and as such, contributes directly to productivity and profit. As a lean business practice, Kaizen succeeds when all employees look for areas to improve and provide suggestions based on their observations and experience. The Kaizen process may use many lean techniques to achieve continuous improvement and include (but are not limited to):

- ○ Automation: Look for processes that can be automated to improve efficiency and make work easier.
- ○ Kanban: Reduce waste by getting the inventory you need, when you need it.
- ○ 5S: Adopt 5S as a system for continuous improvement by achieving facility-wide organization and cleanliness.
- ○ TPM: Eliminate downtime and boost overall production through Total Productive Maintenance.

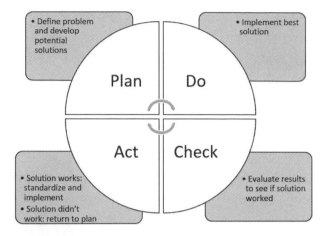

Figure 4-4   *The application of Kaizen follows the cycle of Plan, Do, Check, Act (PDCA)*

For Kaizen to be successful, it must be clear that all suggestions are welcome and that there will be no negative consequences. Toyota, for example rewards employees for changes that improve the workplace. Caterpillar and other large US companies have also embraced this approach. As employee improvements are implemented, work satisfaction is increased and employees become more confident and invested in improving the company.

Kaizen improvements are typically applied by using the cycle Plan, Do, Check, Act (PDCA) as described in Figure 4.4.

PDCA ensures that there is a continuous cycle in place to monitor changes and continue to improve upon them. The overall intent of Kaizen in any organization is to:

- ○ Increase productivity
- ○ Improve quality
- ○ Improve safety
- ○ Lower costs
- ○ Improve customer satisfaction
- ○ Improve communication and cooperation

- ○ Improve morale and employee satisfaction
- ○ Provide greater personal investment in the company among employees and management

As can be seen from this list, the benefits of the Kaizen tool are in direct alignment with the 9 Steps. In other words, by using the Kaizen methodology as part of your 9 Steps, you will be improving upon the business goals of your organization.

We have taken photos and videos of our observations.

Photos and videos of the observations are important for a number of reasons. First, so if team members shift or become unavailable system observations remain consistent and reproducible. Second, so that there is a simple and easily referenced example of a system observation that can be utilized to effectively communicate findings to any key stakeholders or management. And finally, so should system observations change, a comparative "before and after" can be made.

In my experience these photos and videos can be very persuasive as communication tools. They are efficient and practical in meetings, and often pack a more powerful punch than a tedious conversation. They can also be easily sent to team members or stakeholders who may not always be available and suffer from time constraints.

We have created a visual representation or simulation of our observations.

Building a simulation or model of your observations can be an extremely useful tool. Proposed improvements to your system can be simply and more cost-effectively modeled, especially in those instances when your operation is large and/or resource intensive. It is also an effective means of communicating dimensionally, which is often times difficult using only photos or videos which are not easily manipulated.

Prototypes and models of ideas are simple and cost effective means to analyze impacts without making wholesale changes or expending large capital expenditure dollars. With the latest simulation software tools, much can be accomplished by computer. I have seen this approach work especially well in large scale operations where it is just not feasible to make changes due to heavy equipment, massive material quantities or production schedules that simply do not allow for shutdowns.

We have documented our observations.

Documentation is essential to this process, as it is virtually impossible to track either observations, changes, or improvements without it. A clear, systematic approach is important, and there is no need to make it overly complicated. Simple lists and coding will suffice, making sure everything is time and date stamped. Typically, documentation protocol is performed chronologically. However, choose the approach that works best within your system.

I have discovered that the most effective way to make this happen is to assign one single (accountable) person. There are individuals who enjoy doing this type of thing and if they are good at it, let them do it. It is better for an organized, thoughtful, detail-oriented team member to take on this task than it is for the team member who prefers to brainstorm lots of idea with little structure. This is an important and often overlooked part of the process.

We have not biased our observations; they are objective and analytical.

It is important for team members performing system observations to hold each other accountable for unbiased observations. While it may be difficult to remove yourself from "ownership" within your system, it is important to take an analytical and objective approach. If you or your team feel that your observations are biased, then it is important to bring in a third-party, neutral observer. These third party observers can be those very same outside evaluators that perform your RCA, fishbone or Kaizen. These individuals are trained to be unbiased, and due to their third party status are not vested in the internal dynamics of the organization.

It is the responsibility of the team leader to ensure this objectivity and if he/she sees it in any of the team members or observational results, he/she must remove it. It can be culturally problematic at times to overcome bias. Organizational culture can be a strong and steady presence that pulls results in one direction or another. Change agents can be viewed with both fear and distrust, and insiders may approach team members in order to skew results or influence outcomes. Both the team leader and the team itself must be both aware of, and immune to, these influences.

We have organized and filed our observations in a manner that can be easily identified, accessed, and duplicated by others.

Not just the documentation and organization is important, but also the filing of the information. If file folders are not easily named and found within your IT system, it will be virtually impossible for others to utilize your information. As with number 7 above, a systematic approach to keeping the observations and results readily available is an essential part of this step.

We have created a summary presentation of our observations that tie to our business goals.

How many of you have been stuck in meetings or presentations while thinking "get to the point"?

Assume your audience is the same. Don't bore them with endless details. Present your relevant findings, observations, and conclusions. Summarize. Be brief. But get your point across. As a system improvement team, you will only have a few opportunities to get buy-in for your proposed changes. Use them to your advantage. Don't overdo on data. Don't make your audience suffer through the arduous and difficult process that you had to endure. Make it interesting and exciting. Tie each and every part of your presentation to improved business goals.

We have presented our findings to the right audience for feedback.

  ○ *The individuals involved in the system we observed*

  ○ *The appropriate decision-makers*

  ○ *All stakeholders*

Before your summary presentation make sure that you are presenting to the right audience for feedback. Make sure you get the right amount of feedback from all stakeholders including both those individuals involved in the observed system, as well as the appropriate decision-makers. This is the responsibility of the system improvement team leader to make sure you are presenting your findings to the right group. Don't waste either their time or yours.

Our system improvement team leader has approved our observation plan prior to beginning any system observations. Alignment between team members, SMEs, stakeholders, and the team leader is important throughout all 9 Steps. In the case of the observation plan, this is especially important to ensure that both the observation methodology and time and resources used to implement the observations are both available and approved. The system improvement team leader should be in frequent and ongoing communication with management for approval and next steps. The team leader also serves as liaison between the team and decision-makers.

The LEGO Case Study According to Step 4:
Observe the System

Good business decisions do not always seem rational or obvious at first glance. In the LEGO case, Knudstorp and Ovesen spent much of 2003 observing operations, analyzing business centers and products, and reviewing performance of key products and services. Many of Ovesen's observations led to significant changes in the organization over the next few years. Among the initial findings: no profit and loss ledger by product type, no profit and loss by line, and no clear metrics on whether the LEGOLAND parks made or lost money. The company was organized in a matrix hierarchy, whereby twelve senior VP's oversaw only six regions, and to Knudstorp they were operating in silos with little to no accountability to each other or the organization as a whole. New products, new lines, and new tooling were being introduced with little to no analysis of any impacts to the larger system.

Knudstorp, Ovesen and their team were careful to remove any organizational or observational bias, and carefully captured and documented their findings, while simultaneously communicating with key stakeholders in presentations to management. Ovesen specifically used financial analysis tools to quantify these findings and began to develop and implement key performance metrics to observe progress such as line profitability, full manufacturing cost ratios, and return on sales targets.

Step 4	SYSTEM OBSERVATION FORM

SYSTEM DESCRIPTION: ▻

Observation team: leaders	Method/system responsible for	Email	Phone	Due date

Name of analysis tool(s): ▻ _____

▻ (time study, method analysis, brainstorm, RCS, Kaizen, etc.)

Team leader approval: ▻ _____

Signature   Date

Management approval: ▻ _____

Signature   Date

Proposed completion: ▻ (Date) _____

All data, photos, videos, files will be stored in this link: ▻ _____

SUMMARY OF OBSERVATIONS

Analysis tool used: ▻	
Outcomes:	▻
	▻
Analysis tool used: ▻	
Outcomes:	▻
	▻
Analysis tool used: ▻	
Outcomes:	▻
	▻

We will present a summary of our findings to the following stakeholders:

Stakeholder's Name	Position	Email	Phone

OBSERVATION GROUND RULES: ✓

▶ We have communicated our intent to improve the system with all relevant stakeholders

▶ We have properly documented all observations

▶ Our observations are objective and analytical, and not biased

▶ We have organized and filed our observations in a clear manner

▶ We have created a summary presentation of our findings that tie to our business goals

▶ We have presented a summary of our findings to key stakeholders

Step 5:
Identify Bottlenecks within the System

"The entire bottleneck concept is not geared to decrease operating expense, it's focused on increasing throughput."

—Eliyahu M. Goldratt
The Goal

Ensure that the focus of system improvements directly targets those areas that will impact the business goals of the organization most significantly.

Step 5 is built around the Theory of Constraints developed by Eliyahu Goldratt in the early 1980s. Described in the best-selling book *The Goal*, Goldratt identified some base assumptions and conclusions about manufacturing operations that have led to an almost universal change in how many large companies run their processes and identify opportunities for improvement.

While Step 5 is in no way meant to attempt to replicate or change Goldratt's groundbreaking work, it is meant to provide a solid introduction to its principles. For a more detailed and accurate understanding of the Theory of Constraints, you should read *The Goal* and/or visit www.goldratt.com. For the purposes of these 9 Steps, Step 5 is the first step in identifying bottlenecks or problems within the observed system.

According to Goldratt, *The Goal* is about people trying to understand what makes their world tick so that they can make it better. This mindset is no different in organizations. In my experience, most of the employees who I work with across numerous industries *do* want to make their companies better, and most strive for success. While *The Goal* focuses on a manufacturing company, I have found that Goldratt's principles hold true for any product or service. To me, manufacturing is simply a *process*. And every process within any organization is simply a system that can be improved. Whether you provide accounting services, build spaceships or run a hospital, everything you do is some sort of process. What makes the Theory of Constraints unique is the determined focus on throughput—or making money. This focus is the primary reason for the inclusion of the Theory of Constraints into the 9 Steps.

First, it is necessary to provide a brief overview of the principles behind the Theory of Constraints. When *The Goal* was written, the United States was facing the demise of the manufacturing industry because of competition from other countries and the ability to out-source to cheaper facilities. Goldratt believed that applying basic sci-entific principles of cause and effect to business assumptions would allow those assumptions to be challenged. He believed that only by challenging these basic assumptions are breakthroughs possible. 9 Steps takes those principles just a few steps further and provides a singular and simple methodology of "how" to do just that.

Goldratt summarized this quest elegantly at the conclusion of his book with three basic questions:

○ What do we change?
○ What do we change to?
○ How do we cause the change?

The Goal is written as a novel, documenting the story of Alex Rogo, a plant manager whose factory is failing. His operation is shipping orders late, performs inefficiently, and ultimately is losing money. In sum, the business is not sustainable. Meanwhile, Alex's marriage is failing under the pressure of his work situation and his boss has given him three months to turn the plant around or it will close.

This story is the backdrop of all things operational and how Gol-dratt neatly lays out his Theory of Constraints. The concept is

STEP 5—IN THE REAL WORLD

One of the first challenges the Client A team faced was understanding that a fundamental shift in thinking was required to move from job-specific, one-off fabrication processes to a leaner, manufacturing-based process. To understand this shift, the team began by reading *The Goal* by Eliyahu Goldratt. Client A then invited the Goldratt Institute to visit and train the team on the principles of *The Goal* and to help each of them understand and implement the methodology behind it.

Throughout the productivity improvement initiative, team members strove to utilize the terminology and understand that "keeping the field busy" was not necessarily the most productive way to operate business.

The term "bottleneck, constraint or Herbie" was generally understood within the team as that step or process that negatively impacted throughput—or the way their organization made money. As an example, early on, material handling was identified as the bottleneck and adjustments were made to processing whereby materials were delivered by a mobile trailer and stored vertically at the correct location.

The team performed significant analyses and held numerous discussions to ensure that by removing any of these bottlenecks, that they were indeed improving "throughput," and not at the expense of increasing either inventory or operating expense (for example, if delivering the materials vertically actually created a glut of steel sitting in the facility and increased inventory costs, it would not have actually solved the bottleneck and increased throughput). It would, instead, have increased inventory costs.

relatively simple: the success of the plant is solely determined by the bottleneck that constrains overall output. Remember that for the purposes of these 9 Steps a bottleneck is defined as any resource or step within our system where work does not flow to meet demand and could be made more efficient. The same is true for Alex Rogo's plant. In sum, the theory contends that the whole plant can only move as fast as its slowest point. And it does not matter where in the process this bottleneck occurs, nor does it matter who is causing it. It only matters that it is occurring. The solution is simple: All company resources should be directed at eliminating or reducing this bottleneck until you identify and tackle the next, and the next.

This may sound overly obvious, but indeed it is not. In my own experience, I have seen organizations ignore these fundamentals time and time again. In *The Goal*, Goldratt provides the example of Alex pulling workers off of other machines in order to make sure the bottleneck machine is never idle, and receives significant pushback from managers and accounting. This step was taken, despite the fact that the remainder of the plant equipment was producing a non-stop stream of parts that would lie around uselessly until the bottleneck machine could catch up. I see this same thinking even today. Instead of assigning workers to bottlenecks, organizations will assign them to tasks that have nothing to do with either output or throughput (such as ridiculous assignments like cleaning up trash or sorting parts) in order to keep them "busy" and "productive," neither of which they actually are. Most organizations could run in a much leaner and more efficient way by utilizing the very simple principles of the Theory of Constraints and even understanding what makes up a bottleneck.

Goldratt describes just how this works later in the book in his most profound "aha" moment: a hiking trip with his son. As he is hiking with his son's scout troop, Alex notices that the single-file line of scouts never manages to maintain consistent spacing. Instead, the line constantly spreads out, with the fastest kid at the front continually disappearing around the bend and out of sight. At the end of the line Alex, as leader, is stuck with Herbie, the poor little chubby kid who can't keep up. Alex realizes that the group as a whole can only move as fast as Herbie, the poor guy who's constantly causing slowdowns in the middle of the line. And since the goal of the scouting trip is to get all of the kids to the campsite safely, Alex hasn't met his goal until all the kids (including Herbie) have arrived safely.

Alex's solution? He puts Herbie at the front of the line and distributes everything in Herbie's backpack to the other kids, lightening his load. The faster kids then have no problem keeping up with Herbie; Herbie is now faster due to the lighter load, and the system as a whole is improved.

These very same ideas are at the heart of Step 5. More detail and explanation will be provided in each of the steps within the Step 5 checklist to ensure both complete understanding and an ability to put the theory into use.

Each of these steps is important for the following reasons:

We understand that the definition of a bottleneck is any resource or step in our system where work does not flow to meet demand, or could be made more efficient.

Our definition of a bottleneck is consistent with that of *The Goal*, or put more simply, any place within the observed system where a resource requires the longest time to meet demand. Think of traffic, where four lanes are reduced to two, and create slower movement of vehicles through a point in traffic operations. If four lanes were open, then traffic would move through more quickly, but since the available resources were limited, a "bottleneck" occurred and traffic became congested.

For both production and the management of multiple projects, a bottleneck is considered one process in a series of processes that limits the capacity of the entire chain. This bottleneck then results in slowdowns in production, overstock, customer dissatisfaction and low employee morale because of increased internal pressure. For the 9 Steps, short-term bottlenecks such as employees on vacation or a delayed delivery are not normally considered significant enough to tackle as an issue.

The same principle holds true for any process within any business, large or small. For any organization, identifying bottlenecks is critical to improving efficiency. And usually the first place to look is any place where accumulation occurs. Any business process that accumulates the longest wait time is usually, but not always, the bottleneck.

Accumulation is defined as any point within your system where a buildup of work or slowdown of process can be identified that results from the next point's inability to meet capacity. If you have a series of processes within your system, and any one of them could be a bottleneck, then a fishbone diagram can be a very effective way to identify all of the possible problems within a chain of processes. As described in Step 4, the fishbone tool is extremely effective for collecting all of the data, inputting it into the diagram, and then analyzing the diagram to identify the root cause of the problem.

The concept here, while it may sound complicated, is actually quite simple: once you have identified the system that you wish to improve within your business, and have observed the work within it, you must now identify that single bottleneck that most impacts your business goals negatively. In other words, find that one thing that if fixed, will give you the largest return for your time, resources, and effort.

We understand that the terms "bottleneck, constraint, and Herbie" can be used interchangeably.

From time to time, you may hear the terms "bottleneck, constraint or Herbie." For the purposes of these 9 Steps, these terms are used interchangeably. As described in the overview of Goldratt's *The Goal*, Alex Rogo went on a scouting trip and was able to identify Herbie as the bottleneck or constraint in the hiking progression. While some may argue that a bottleneck and a constraint are arguably different (a constraint can be called a bottleneck but a bottleneck is not always a constraint), for our purposes they remain the same.

STEP 5 CHECKLIST

- We understand that the definition of a bottleneck is any resource or step in our system where work does not flow to meet demand, or could be made more efficient.

- We understand that the terms "bottleneck, constraint, and Herbie" can be used interchangeably.

- Our team has relied on our observations and experience to identify the bottlenecks in our system.

- We have identified where a bottleneck exists based upon an accumulation of work in progress (a point where work has stopped or slowed).

- We have identified the underlying root causes that have contributed to this bottleneck.

- We have identified the impact of our bottleneck on:
  - Throughput—the rate at which we generate money
  - Inventory—facilities, equipment, obsolete items, raw material, work-in-progress, finished goods
  - Operating expense—direct labor, utilities, consumables, supplies, depreciation of assets

- We understand that the goal of our system improvement is to maximize throughput while minimizing inventory and operating expense.

- We understand all interdependencies between and across our system and its processes

- We have verified our observed bottlenecks by performing the appropriate mathematical evaluation to ensure they are bottlenecks.

***Our team has relied on our observations and experience to
identify the bottlenecks in our system.***

Once again, Picking the Right Team (Step 2) is critical to the process. This will enable your group to much more efficiently and
expertly identify any existing problems within your system. Often
your team may know where these bottlenecks or constraints exist
without much prompting, and this can be a straightforward place
to start.

Another effective means to identify the top bottlenecks is to ask
those working within the system, since their hands-on knowledge
can quickly identify areas of frustration. In many instances, the people doing the work within the system will know exactly where to go
to identify accumulation. They will know exactly where the pain
points exist; they'll be happy to tell you all about it.

I worked with one company that sold acoustic ceiling tiles. It was
a subcontractor to several of the largest commercial real estate devel-
opers in the Southwest. I had been hired to help the firm improve its
profit margin, as year after year it limped by with little to show for
its efforts. The company was owned by a man and his wife, who had
built the business from the ground up and still ran everything with
an iron fist. The company had grown significantly over the last
twenty years; yet, despite all of its growth, the owners were making
less than they had some ten years earlier.

Something just wasn't working; the owners knew it, I knew it,
and it was time to find out why. This was one of those situations
where the owners had a gut instinct that something was failing but
they could not put their fingers on exactly what it was. Upon reviewing the historical financial report, we determined that the system
that needed improvement was job gain (average margin across all
jobs after installation). The last five years of operation saw a steady
decline in gain, coupled with a steady increase in overhead which is
a sure formula for profit erosion. But why?

We assembled a team of staff engineers and job site craftsmen to discuss their observations and identify what they thought could be contributing to the problem. Something was happening somewhere in the process that caused a disconnect between the guys designing the installation and the guys installing it. It took about ten minutes before the installation superintendent said, "The problem is that every time we get a drawing from the office, we basically ignore it because we know it will be wrong."

Heads at the table whipped around to look at him in surprise. The owner was sitting there, and I think everyone was shocked the guy had the guts to say something like this in front of him. The design engineers immediately started shuffling papers and talking over him, but it didn't take long for the owner to say, "Let him speak, I want to hear more."

The superintendent went on to describe how every time he got a drawing, he would have to call the office four of five times to clarify one dimension or another, and he spent more time calling the office than he did installing any ceilings. He explained that sometimes he would wait for as long as a half hour for the engineers to call him before he could even get his crews working. He said this happened so often that the guys stood around about 25 percent of their day waiting for information.

The owner was shocked. He could not believe that he was paying his labor force to stand around 25 percent of their day, and said so in the meeting. In this case, the bottleneck was not the crews not installing fast enough, but the lack of accurate information from the design group. And the guys installing the ceiling tiles knew it. They knew exactly what was happening and why they were slow. It only took assembling the right team to figure it out. Had we met only with management or just the engineers, there is no way we would have known what was really going on.

We have identified where a bottleneck exists based upon an accumulation of work in progress (a point where work has stopped or slowed).

An easy means of identifying a bottleneck within a system is to simply observe where within the system that work has accumulated or slowed. (Examples: documents piled on a desk, fitters waiting on welders, workers waiting on materials, tools unavailable, and so forth.) These visual cues are often highly representative of the most egregious constraints. In most project-based organizations, multiple projects are occurring simultaneously and there are resources that must be shared between and among projects. There are also only so many capable and talented people to go around and managing projects to budgets and schedules becomes increasingly difficult. That's why it may not be as simple as identifying a single point of constraint.

Types of constraints can include:

- Equipment: Equipment utilization limits the ability of the system to produce more salable goods/services.
- People: Lack of skilled people limits the system. Individual behaviors can also become a constraint.
- Policy: A written or unwritten policy prevents the system from producing more salable goods/services.

The only way to tackle this issue is to rely on Step 1: Identifying the System that Needs Improvement. This is the only way to clearly identify what you want to fix *within your predetermined system boundaries*. In other words, eat the elephant one bite at a time.

We have identified the underlying root causes that have contributed to this bottleneck.

It is not sufficient to simply identify that single point within your system that is a constraint to your operational throughput (or productivity) but to both identify and understand the root causes that contributed to this bottleneck. You can either utilize a formal tool such as TapRoot, Root Cause Analysis (RCA), fishbone diagrams or others (as described in both Step 4 and Appendix C), but the purpose of such an exercise is to find those common denominators contributing to slowdown within the system. (Examples include change management process, lack of standard processes, roles and responsibilities are not clearly defined, lack of communication, etc.)

The only way to fix the bottleneck is to change or improve the underlying root causes. In the paint damage example in Step 4, the paint damage had been identified as a bottleneck within an assembly system (so much damage was occurring that repairing the damage was slowing the final assembly) and several underlying root causes were identified:

- No initial audit for bad quality paint
- No initial audit for incorrect paint
- Packaging not conducive to protecting paint
- Sub not notified of proper paint instruction
- Sub not notified of changes

Only now can the system improvement team focus on that optimal solution that will most positively impact the business goals of their organization. And they can do this because they have identified the root causes and can now methodically and analytically eliminate that one (or more) that is contributing the most to the bottleneck, and ultimately impacting profit the most.

We have identified the impact of our bottleneck on:

- *Throughput*
- *Inventory*
- *Operating expense*

In order to fully utilize the Theory of Constraints, and the thinking behind the model, it is important to fully understand the whole system and the impacts of the bottlenecks both within and upon it.

For business, inventory is all the money that the system has invested in purchasing those things which it intends to sell; operating expense is all the money the system spends to turn inventory into throughput, and throughput is simply the rate at which the system generates money. We will more thoroughly define these below in an attempt to make sure this premise is clearly understood. For without subjugation to throughput, the 9 Steps process will not work.

There are several key definitions in the Theory of Constraints. I have heard several other terms used interchangeably for throughput: profit, gain, margin, velocity, and productivity to name a few. No matter what the terminology is, as long as it means "making money," the terminology is relevant. Without a full grasp of these definitions, it is difficult to fully realize and quantify overall system improvements. These definitions in detail are:

- Throughput = the rate at which your organization generates money

- Inventory = facilities, equipment, obsolete items just laying around, raw materials, work currently in progress, all finished goods

- Operating expense = cost of your direct labor, utilities, consumable supplies, depreciation of existing assets

Don't be overly concerned with the complexities of the Theory of Constraints for the purpose of the 9 Steps. I have selected those applications that are most relevant to this process. The Theory of Constraints contains much more (Drum Buffer Rope and so on) but these concepts are not critical to the 9 Steps process. What *is* critical is the ability to fully grasp the relevance of both bottlenecks and throughput to your organization and how to tie them to the ultimate outcome of improving the business goals of your company.

We understand that the goal of our system improvement is to maximize throughput while minimizing inventory and operating expense.

The goal of any system improvement includes the maximization of throughput (making money) while **simultaneously** minimizing inventory and operating expense. In other words, it is not good enough to just reduce inventory and/or operating expenses (such as cutting costs, trimming overhead); you must **also** maximize throughput within your system.

As an example, if you were able to increase pipe supply throughput (fabrication) after identifying a bottleneck, but it resulted in increased inventory (pipes sitting around in the facility but not scheduled for installation), then you have actually **reduced** the positive impact on the business. Let's use an example of a store that sells guitars. The throughput of that store would be all the guitars that are sold. The inventory in that store would include all of the guitar store facilities, equipment, and all the guitars that remain unsold in the building. The operating expenses of the guitar store would include the salespeople and managers, the lights and water, and all of the supplies needed to keep the store running.

If the manager decided that he wanted to increase throughput (sell more guitars) and he decided to stock more colorful and popular guitars in order to attract more people, then this approach would only be considered successful if he made more profit at the end of the day (AFTER subtracting the cost of his inventory). If, however, he sold more guitars, but the cost of having ten additional colorful guitars in inventory overshadowed this gain, then it was not a successful improvement.

We understand all interdependencies between and across our system and its processes.

Understanding the interdependencies between and across your system and its processes is a vital element of system improvement.

Organizations suffer from severe inefficiencies when these interdependencies are not fully understood.

For example, how many projects have you been on where 100 percent completion is the goal of your section of the job, yet when it comes time to hand off to the next department or discipline you are not at 100 percent? Still, the handoff is made and disciplines end up performing in an entirely inefficient and out-of-sequence manner. Keep in mind that *every single* operation has costs associated with it, and both upstream and downstream interdependencies can greatly influence these costs.

Some of these interdependencies include:

○ Vendors
○ Subcontractors
○ Warehouse
○ Other departments
○ Other projects competing for resources
○ Equipment availability
○ Availability of qualified personnel

All of the above should be monitored and tracked as part of the overall system improvement. Additionally, each should be considered when sketching out any fishbone diagrams or other root cause analyses as possible contributors.

We have verified our observed bottlenecks by performing the appropriate mathematical evaluation to ensure they are bottlenecks.

It is important to verify that those bottlenecks or constraints that you have identified are indeed constraints within your system and that the impacts to your system can be mathematically and/or quantitatively proven. Working solely from assumption or anecdotal information is not sufficient; while this approach can be used to initially identify that a bottleneck could exist, empirical verification is necessary before proceeding to Step 6.

The LEGO Case Study According to Step 5:
Identify Bottlenecks within the System

While the Ashcroft case study does not specifically utilize Theory of Constraints language, some of the principles remain the same. The purpose of identifying any bottlenecks within the system or organization is to identify those constraints within the system that are most negatively impacting the business goals of that organization. In the LEGO case, Knudstorp identified the LEGO diversification strategy (which included software, learning concepts, lifestyle products, girls' toys, books, magazines, television, theme parks, and brand retail) as the single largest bottleneck to profitability within the organization. Each of these strategies within LEGO demanded a specialized skill set and took capital, time, and resources away from the core LEGO business.

According to Knudstorp, "... there were basically two fundamental challenges that grew out of this period—over-stretching and overexpansion." Knudstorp and his team, once landing on this organizational bottleneck, then spent the next two years resolving this bottleneck to stabilize business and restore profitability. Remaining focused on the goal of their improvement effort was key to their eventual success. And it was this fairly early identification of a fundamental bottleneck that enabled Knudstorp and his team to take the next steps. If we were to interpret the LEGO Case Study in purely Theory of Constraints terminology, we could assume the following:

- ○ Throughput—the rate at which LEGO generated profits

- Inventory—all LEGO facilities, equipment, work-in-progress, and products

- Operating Expense—all LEGO direct labor, utilities, consumables, supplies, and depreciation of assets

Clearly, Knudstorp and his team realized that the only way to improve Throughput (profit) for LEGO, was to maximize profit, while simultaneously reducing inventory (non-profitable facilities, work and products) and operating expenses associated with these products. And while Theory of Constraints is most commonly associated with manufacturing processes, it is easy to see that it is applicable to any system that produces work.

Step 5	IDENTIFY THE BOTTLENECK FORM

KEY DEFINITIONS:

THROUGHPUT
The rate at which we generate revenue

INVENTORY
Facilities, equipment, obsolete items, raw material, work-in-progress, finished goods

OPERATING EXPENSE
Direct labor, utilities, consumables, supplies, depreciation of assets

BOTTLENECK/CONSTRAINT/HERBIE
Any resource or step in the system where work does not flow to meet demand

ROOT CAUSE
The fundamental reason for the occurence of a bottleneck

Techniques used to identify bottlenecks:

▶ Experience of our experts:	▶
	▶
	▶
▶ Gut feel/instinct:	▶
	▶
	▶
▶ Observations of accumulated work-in-progress/inefficiencies:	▶
	▶
	▶
▶ Observations of work within system that is behind schedule:	▶
	▶
This bottleneck impacts (may be one or more):	▶
Throughput:	▶
Inventory:	▶
Operating Expense:	▶

Step 5 cont'd	IDENTIFY THE BOTTLENECK FORM

Tool utilized to identify the Root Cause of the bottleneck:
(RCA, Kaizen, fishbone, brainstorm, etc.)

▶ _____

Top 3 Root Causes of Bottleneck:	Analytical/Mathematical Tools Used to Verify the validity of identified bottlenecks:
1.	1.
2.	2.
3.	3.

MATHEMATICAL OUTCOMES:
(show your work)

Management Approval:

_____   _____
Signature   Date

We understand that the goal of our system improvement
is to maximize throughput while minimizing inventory and operating expense.

Step 6:
Brainstorm

"It takes two to speak the truth—one to speak,
and another to hear."

—Henry David Thoreau
A Week on the Concord and Merrimack Rivers

Utilize the right team to accumulate a list of the best possible solutions for improvement to the system.

Step 6 is that intersection within the process whereby your system improvements will either be truly innovative or otherwise sink into the quagmire of recycled ideas. Much has been written on the brainstorming process, and many high tech organizations pride themselves on their abilities to reinvent themselves at will. Often big ideas are a stumbled upon by accident.

> *A man on an assembly line accidentally discovered Saran Wrap by "blowing bubbles" with an air compressor. The first thing it wrapped was machine guns.*

> *The inventors of **ASTROTURF** thought they had the perfect solution for the shortage of playground space in urban areas. They would cover every city rooftop and let the kids play on the tops of their building.*

According to Ed Engoron, CEO of Perspectives Inc., a think-tank for the food industry and creator of many food innovations at Disney, Taco Bell, and McDonalds, most "Big Ideas" start out as little ideas, notions, or seeds of concepts.

The process of ideation, however, does not come naturally to most of us. Our experience teaches us, from a very young age, that there are right ways to do things and wrong ways to do things; that there are right answers and wrong answers; and even that there *are* stupid questions . . . despite what your peers or superiors tell you. Is there any wonder then that most of us are ill-prepared to participate in a no-holds-barred, positive interchange of ideas in which you are encouraged to dream and play "I wish for" games?

According to Robert Sutton in *Hard Facts, Dangerous Half-Truths and Total Nonsense: Profiting from Evidence-Based Management*, group brainstorming isn't perfect even when it is done well. When brainstorming sessions are managed appropriately and skillfully linked to other work practices, such gatherings can promote innovation. He established eight guidelines that are especially important for running effective face-to-face brainstorms.

Sutton's Guidelines for Face-to-Face Brainstorms[*]

1. Use brainstorming to combine and extend ideas, not just to harvest ideas.

Andrew Hargadon's *How Breakthroughs Happen* shows that creativity occurs when people find ways to build on existing ideas. The power of group brainstorming comes from creating a safe place where people with different ideas can share, blend, and extend their diverse knowledge. The use of tools like Real Time Board can help this process immensely.

2. **Don't bother if people live in fear.**

   As Sigmund Freud observed, groups bring out the best and worst in people. If people believe they will be teased, paid less, demoted, fired, or otherwise humiliated, group brainstorming is a bad idea.

3. **Do individual brainstorming before and after group sessions.**

   Alex Osborn's 1950s classic *Applied Imagination*, which popularized brainstorming, gave advice that is still sound: creativity comes from a blend of the individual and collective "ideation." Skilled organizers tell participants what the topic will be before a brainstorm.

4. **Brainstorming sessions are worthless unless they are woven with other work practices.**

   Brainstorming is just one of the many practices that make a company creative;it is of little value if it's not combined with other practices—such as observing users, talking to experts, or building prototype products or experiences—that provide an outlet for the ideas generated.

5. **Brainstorming requires skill and experience both to do and, especially, to facilitate.**

   At Hewlett-Packard's SAP's Design Services Team, brainstorming is treated as a skill that takes months or years to master. Facilitating a session is a skill that takes even longer to develop. If you hold brainstorms every now and then, and they are led by people without skill and experience, don't be surprised if participants "sit there looking embarrassed."

6. **A good brainstorming session is competitive—in the right way.**

   In the best brainstorms, people feel pressure to show off what they know and how skilled they are at building on others' ideas. But people are also competitive in a paradoxical way. The worst thing a manager can do is set up the session as an "I win, you lose" game in which ideas are explicitly rated, ranked, and rewarded.

7. **Use brainstorming sessions for more than just generating good ideas.**

   Brainstorms aren't just a place to generate good ideas. At IDEO, these gathering support the company's culture and work practices in a host of other ways. Project teams use brainstorms to get inputs from people with diverse skills throughout the company. In the process, a lot of other good things happen. Knowledge is spread about new industries and technologies, newcomers and veterans learn—or are reminded—about who knows what, and jumping into a brainstorm for an hour or so to think about someone else's problem provides a welcome respite from the designers' own projects.

8. **Follow the rules, or don't call it a brainstorm.**

   The worst "brainstorms" happen when the term is used loosely, and the rules aren't followed—or known—at all. Perhaps the biggest mistake that leaders make is failing to keep their mouths shut.

   The rules vary from place to place. But Alex Osborne's original four still work: don't allow criticism, encourage wild ideas, go for quantity, combine and/or improve on others' ideas.

Brainstorming is a key element of the 9 Steps process. It is virtually impossible in today's economy for organizations to grow without innovation—using new concepts and new ideas. Most business professionals and many management thought leaders agree that innovation is critical to success. Recent studies reveal that more than ninety percent of executives believe that long-term success is directly linked to the organizations ability to develop new ideas. Despite this awareness at the top, many employees feel that their company is simply not doing enough to nurture this way of thinking. And the problem lies in that neither know how. Executives and managers understand the need, and employees want to contribute, but neither know how to do so in a systematic, results-driven manner.

There are two killers of effective brainstorming sessions: bias and groupthink. Bias is the desire to stick to the status quo and it is driven primarily by fear. Although this type of fear of change can often be unfounded, psychological research indicates that this type of bias is a "go to" reflex that many humans display. This knee-jerk reaction is not at all conducive to innovation or the brainstorming process, and can also explain why even though good ideas can be generated, it is often difficult to actually implement them. This becomes especially difficult the more radical (and often riskier) the idea. The higher the risk, the easier it is for the supervisor to say no. If your organization displays this type of status quo bias, it may be difficult to foster creativity and promote brainstorming. It will also become difficult to create a culture of continuous change or improvement the more "stuck" your organizational culture.

Groupthink is the second deadliest enemy of brainstorming. Groupthink is defined as achieving consensus while minimizing conflict. In a groupthink environment, conflict avoidance is the primary goal over achieving any breakthrough in thought. Groupthink can be an end-result of status quo bias, or it can be a reflection of heavy-handed management. Either way, groupthink suppresses innovation and individual thought. Organizations that exhibit groupthink culture often miss market shifts or miss out on new technologies. Organizations with strong process history also tend to groupthink internal processes, as straying from these paths can be viewed as perilous to ongoing operations. Instead, companies continue to use outdated or inefficient processes (or systems) simply because the dread of changing to something new outweighs the perceived value of anything new.

Groupthink can often result in disaster. Overlooking key design flaws in the space shuttle Challenger led to one of the worst accidents in NASA history. In that situation, a small, isolated group involved in a critical decision-making process ignored several key pieces of information. I have personally witnessed this same effect. One of my clients had a project located in a very remote location. Employees worked shifts of three weeks on and two weeks off. During their three weeks on, employees lived in what was called the job "camp." This camp included living quarters, a sparse dining hall and store, and a tiny, winding roadway up the side of a mountain. It was not an easy place to get to, nor was it a particularly pleasant place to live. As such, employees very much looked forward to getting out of there and heading back to their families at the end of their shifts.

One Friday afternoon the weather was bad. The shift was over and everyone was tired and wanted to go home. Despite weather warnings, the group of employees was able to convince the bus driver to head down the mountain. They had all become friends over the months and the bus driver did not want to disappoint the team and make them lose any of their time off, despite his reservations about driving in such inclement weather. So off they went down the mountain, almost zero visibility, surrounded by whipping wind and snow. The pressure of this groupthink cost the bus driver and all seven people their lives.

Avoiding both bias and groupthink is essential to Step 6 and two checklists are provided to ensure that neither occurs.

There are many types of innovation strategies:

- *Breakthrough:* developing completely new ideas or concepts without relying on previous concepts. Example: new technology.

- *Incremental:* small, minor step-by-step improvements to an existing system or technology. Example: a newer model car.

○ *Disruptive:* typically developed in a niche market, not usually popular at first, but gains popularity due to ease of use. Example: cell phones.

○ *Open:* using both internal and external resources to develop new ideas. Example: focus groups for new technology.

Step 6 utilizes the "open" innovation concept model and suggests that this type of innovation is the least costly and most effective way to introduce new ideas and generate fresh concepts within your organization. The Step 6 Checklist is designed to assist in removing any barriers, and help guide your organization to not only do things well, but continuously seek to do them better.

STEP 6 CHECKLIST

- Our system improvement team has developed a culture that promotes innovation, ideas, and brainstorming.
- Our team avoids bias. (Bias Checklist)
- Our team avoids groupthink. (Groupthink Checklist)
- We understand that avoiding bias and groupthink will increase our team's innovation.
- We have considered examples of benchmarking and best practices from both inside and outside our organization.
- We have allowed for innovative and creative ideas that may sound crazy at the time.
- We shut down any negativity around creative thought.
- We have documented our brainstorming efforts.
- Our ideas will increase the capacity of our identified bottlenecks and positively impact the performance of our system.
- Our brainstorming ideas are aligned with the business goals of our organization.

Our system improvement team has developed a culture that promotes innovation, ideas, and brainstorming.

The team you assembled in Step 2 (Put the Right Team Together) must continuously and consistently develop and promote a culture of innovation that will allow for both incremental improvements as well as "crazy thinking." These individuals must be both the champions and the stewards of this approach to thinking, as well as hold both regular members and outside-the-network attendees accountable to the brainstorming ground rules (Bias and Groupthink Checklists).

The role of the team leader is vital in this process. If the team leader is unable to challenge, promote, and foster creativity among team members, then that person is not right for the job. I have observed many "brainstorming" sessions become filibusters led by meeting leaders who insist that their views, ideas, and observations are the only items worth mentioning or of any value. It is also perfectly acceptable to hold unscheduled meetings, to get together when inspiration hits, to not "force" good ideas or novel ways of doing things. To come up with novel concepts, try running your discussions in a novel manner or at a new location or venue. Grant team members time to go away and think. Get away from the office. Take field trips. Try something new.

I have seen this work very well. Once a client took the system improvement team to a new city altogether. While there, the team toured several companies, none of which offered products or services remotely related to their business. A couple of these visits were with state-of-the-art emerging technology firms. Some of the younger employees (who were subsequently much more open to the use of new software applications) saw potential for use within their own business processes. The trip opened their eyes to many possibilities they had never considered. This was an example of "you don't know what you don't know" and the feeling of excitement from the group was palpable. I remember the team leader eyeing me across the room during one of these tours. A barely imperceptible nod was all that was needed to confirm that we had ignited the creative flames.

Our team avoids bias. (see Bias Checklist)

The two checklists (Bias and Groupthink) list the ground rules for the brainstorming sessions. It is the responsibility of the team leader to review these ground rules with the team members, as well as hold them accountable when they are exhibiting either bias or groupthink. The Bias Checklist can be utilized as a simple and effective tool for avoiding any individual, organizational or cultural bias during the brainstorming process. It is recommended that team leaders utilize this checklist during every brainstorming session as a compass to guide them through the process.

Bias Checklist:

- I am not in love with the idea because it is my idea.
- We do not like the idea because we finally decided on an idea, any idea.
- We did not decide on this idea because the loudest person in the room championed it.
- We did not pick this idea only because it was successful in the past.
- We did not pick this idea because the owner of the idea has had success in the past.
- We did not pick this idea based on unsubstantiated data, numbers or metrics.
- We did not pick this idea because it will be the cheapest to implement.
- We did not pick this idea because we know management will approve it.
- We selected this idea because it was the best idea.

As can be seen from the Bias Checklist, the questions are designed to prompt the team to rely not on history, experience, tenure, position, title, behavior or volume, but instead to focus on ideas with merit, regardless of originator.

I am not in love with the idea because it is my idea: This is classic confirmation bias, the kind that senior executives often fall prey to. It essentially means you are more likely to seek (and find) information that confirms what you already believe. This is not to say that you should forego passion. Passion is the genesis of many good (and sometimes great) ideas. Just remember to gut check yourself. If others on your team are not quite as enthusiastic about your idea, it may be a sign.

We do not like the idea because we finally decided on an idea, any idea: If you have ever sat in a meeting that has gone in circles, then you understand the need for this ground rule. Never, ever simply settle for an idea because you are tired, bored, overwhelmed, resigned, or want to get out of the meeting. If this happens, you have several choices: adjourn and start again another day, capture any ideas that seem of merit and re-examine them later, or reassemble a different team.

We did not decide on this idea because the loudest person in the room championed it: As mentioned previously, there are "talkers" and there are "listeners" in every meeting. Just because someone speaks either more frequently, more loudly, or more insistently than any other member of the team, this does not translate to idea value. Weigh ideas on the merit of the idea, not the person advocating it. Innovation is an iterative process and should include the input and voice of all involved.

We did not pick this idea only because it was successful in the past: There may be times when it is tempting to use tried-and-true success stories from the past. This can be especially relevant when members of the system improvement team come from other departments or other companies and bring those processes and systems with them. Avoid this bias, and make sure to vet ideas in the context of your system and your value (and how it ultimately ties back to your business goals). Remember that the business goals of another organization may have been different, and that these ideas or improvements may not be in alignment with your company's goals.

We did not pick this idea because the owner of the idea has had success in the past: Another temptation is to rely heavily on those who have been successful in coming up with ideas in the past to come up with all ideas for the future. Keep both your team and your own mind open to the possibility that ideas can come from just about anywhere and from just about anyone. There is an interesting duality about this concept; those who have been innovative in the past should certainly be invited to be members of your team, but at the same time do not overvalue their input.

We did not pick this idea based on unsubstantiated data, numbers or metrics: The brainstorming process is designed to be free-flowing and inventive with little to no restrictions on content. However, at some point during the brainstorming process you and your team will need to whittle down the list of ideas into those that are both relevant and positively impact your business goals. Once this list has been narrowed, now you will need to perform a gut check as to whether the idea is realistic, as well as measurable.

We did not pick this idea because it will be the cheapest to implement: I have often attended meetings where ideas get shot down because the expense of testing the idea seems cost-prohibitive. If a wholesale system change is required that will ultimately require significant capital and time, then it is imperative that the team devise a way to develop a prototype or model. I have seen this approach work very well on numerous occasions. For one client, they wanted to test a new laser technology. The cost of the laser system was in the millions and management did not want to purchase a new system that may or may not work within the context of their processes. So the system improvement team rolled up their sleeves and figured out a way to test a scaled-down version.

Additionally, they were able to convince the manufacturer of the laser system to develop the smaller version with them. It worked to the benefit of both. The company was able to prove out the new technology at a much lower cost, and the manufacturer still made the sale. In another case, one of my start-up ventures had a new heat exchanger technology with applications to huge power plants. Their very first customer did not want to purchase the entire system (which would require a multimillion dollar investment) without a preliminary feasibility test. The answer? A desktop model of the system. Simple, cost-effective and effective. In sum, this is a very important ground rule. Remember that if the idea will ultimately improve the business goals of the organization (most importantly profit) then the cost of implementation is irrelevant. (You will be able to prove this using the Return on Investment analysis in Step 7).

We did not pick this idea because we know management will approve it: Often management can either overtly or covertly influence the selection of ideas. I have witnessed the mere presence of a manager in the room shifting both the dynamics of the conversation and the behavior of the participants. And he or she does not need to say a word for this to occur. Sometimes the best ideas will generate the most change. The best ideas can also impact the old way of doing things, as well as the owners of those ways of doing things. Do not be tempted to select an idea because if will be the easiest to get approval for, instead champion your ideas and utilize all 9 Steps to prove their merit.

We selected this idea because it was the best idea: While this ground rule may seem overly obvious, the intention is that the system improvement team generally agree the final selection is the *best* idea, not the simplest, the cheapest, the most appealing to management, or the only one the team could ultimately agree to.

Our team avoids groupthink. (see Groupthink Checklist)

As with the Bias Checklist, the Groupthink Checklist is also designed to help guide the brainstorming team to avoid the pitfalls of groupthink, a behavioral anomaly within organizations that can lead to productivity stalemates and frustration on the part of those fearful of challenging the status quo.

One important item of note on the Groupthink Checklist is your team must challenge not only the answers it comes up with, but ultimately whether the team is asking the correct *questions*. A simple, yet effective, tool that any team leader can use is to simply ask the group at the conclusion of each brainstorming session "have we asked the right questions?" It can also be extremely valuable to ask that very same question of those individuals actually doing the work within the system. They are the audience least likely to be defensive when asked this question.

Groupthink Checklist:

- We have challenged where our data comes from.
- We have challenged whether our metrics are correct.
- We have challenged whether our proposed changes are in alignment with the business goals of the organization and will increase the capacity of our bottleneck.
- We do not assume our questions are correct, and we have asked those questions that identify the correct root causes.
- We do not assume our answers are correct, and we have consensus within our team and from the appropriate stakeholders that these are the correct answers.

We have challenged where our data comes from: A common psychological behavior when operating in groups is to assume that the information provided by others within your peer group is accurate and objective. The reality is that this is not always the case. I find similarities between groupthink and mass hysteria, especially when system improvement ideas revolve around change and elicit fear. Like mass hysteria, many factors contribute to groupthink, including mass media, rumors, anxiety or excitement, organizational beliefs, internal politics, and management or authority behavior. Do you remember how in 1938, a live fictional radio program by Orson Welles was able to convince the American listening audience that they were being invaded by Martians who were attacking with heat rays and poison gas? This type of collective delusion is absolutely possible when trying to change or improve how your organization operates. If, however, you are able to consistently and systematically challenge all of your assumptions and where your information originates, then this can be avoided.

We have challenged whether our metrics are correct: Metrics are simply numbers that relay important information about the system improvement under question. Both the baseline (before the improvement) and the results (after the improvement) are important, and it is critical that your team is comparing baseline metrics to post-change effects as apples to apples. Usually measuring improvements with one metric is not enough. A combination of metrics should be used and a clear understanding of whether they are the "right" metrics is key to success. You should always use either operational (performance in production or service that tracks the people performing the operation) or financial metrics (that judge the ability of an organization to convert operational performance into profit). Metrics form both the basis of control and make the process objective.

We have challenged whether our proposed changes are in alignment with the business goals of the organization and will increase the capacity of our bottleneck: Another important criteria to evaluate whether your brainstorming idea is indeed the "best" idea is to consider whether, if implemented, it will ultimately increase the capacity of the bottleneck (as described in Step 5) as well as improve the identified business goals (safety, quality, profit, etc.). For example, the team may come up with an excellent suggestion to reduce material costs for production (purchase from an overseas supplier) but if that idea ultimately results in decreased quality, then it is not in alignment with the business goals. The team must constantly challenge all impacts to the overall system and whether suggested improvements will meet the criteria of alignment with all business goals.

We do not assume our questions are correct, and we have asked those questions that identify the correct root causes: A very simple way to meet this ground rule criteria is to review the results of Steps 4 and 5 during the brainstorming sessions. Take a hard look at what your observations told you, review the outcome of your fishbone (or other tool) analysis, and link your brainstorm ideas back to whether or not they address what your system observations indicated. If your brainstorm ideas are wildly off-topic, and are not directly linked to the objective data provided by your analysis, then it may be time to regroup.

We do not assume our answers are correct, and we have consensus within our team and from the appropriate stakeholders that these are the correct answers: At the end of the brainstorming process, it is always a good idea to run your final answers by a team of objective AND vested parties. This reality check can be important, as often the system improvement team can become convinced that the "best" idea is the only idea worth pursuing as a result of functioning in a team vacuum.

STEP 6—IN THE REAL WORLD

One of the single most important steps for Client A's unit rate reduction initiative was to actually change the way the company "thought" about things. In fact, a more formalized Step 6 was created as a result of a manager's frustration with the same ideas coming full-cycle year after year that had little or no relevance to profitability. Often, equipment was being purchased based upon faulty input, or incorrect analysis, or even without consideration for the actual impacts upon the operation. Decisions were being made in a vacuum, by the same small handful of people, because "that's the way we used to do it," or because someone figured keeping craft workers busy during slow periods was the only way to do things.

The brainstorming process for the structural productivity group was critical to its success. They challenged themselves to continuously think of new and different ways of doing things, to not let the same people come up with the same tired ideas, to not let senior people force ideas and decisions on younger, newer people, to let craft weigh in with equal merit. A superintendent ended up becoming the key innovator of the group—and drove the group towards new ways of thinking. Craft teammates were essential to reviewing and analyzing any new ideas with an eye towards those that would ultimately make money. Much of their success can be found in his empowerment of the team and allowing ideas and implementation concepts to flourish.

Together, this team avoided both bias and groupthink and the end results were staggering in their positive financial implications for the company.

We understand that avoiding bias and groupthink will increase our team's innovation.

Listening isn't just about hearing; it requires the willingness to entertain others' viewpoints, especially opposing ones. You must develop your skills as a system team leader for detecting distortion and cross-check information by consulting sources that are inclined to take a different viewpoint. Coming up with the "best" new idea gets tougher every year. The usual competitive analysis may not work when technology shifts ever so rapidly. Opportunities to devise your industry game changers can appear and disappear in the blink of an eye, and everything you do can become fodder for the internet. Innovation requires more than just good analytics. It requires sorting and sifting through enormous quantities of information and data, then developing and shaping options to decide on the best choice. Both imagination and diverse insights come into play, and the team must constantly shift and adapt.

We have considered examples of benchmarking and best practices from both inside and outside our organization.

Benchmarking and best practices are some of the best methods to introduce not just new ideas, but also ideas that have been tested and found to be successful in related industries. Benchmarking is simply a systematic comparison of those systems and processes within other companies in comparison to your own. The benchmarking process, if done well, can reveal performance gaps. However, it is important for the system improvement team to carefully analyze the best practices of other companies in the context of your own company's culture and situation. Make sure to identify in advance what it is you wish to learn about, why you want to learn about it, and what you plan to do with the information once you gain it. It is not enough to simply capture the data and performance statistics of the other firm, but the *how* of their processes. What is different about their system application? Their people? Their culture?

Recently I traveled with a group of engineers and managers to Caterpillar to observe and review their "kitting" process—a tool and material supply process that enabled assembly labor to efficiently and productively fabricate and assemble their work by always ensuring they had the proper tools, materials, and information. My client was not a manufacturing company, nor was it in a business remotely similar to Caterpillar, but it did have employees who needed the proper tools, materials and information. Our tour was fascinating. The plant was spotless, the employees were gracious, and the logistics seamless. Caterpillar had completely overhauled its own internal processes, and the results were impressive. The integration of the warehousing and assembly was by far one of the best practices I had ever witnessed. My client ended up taking much of what it learned form that tour and successfully incorporating it into its own work packaging.

There are also industry groups that get together to share best practices, even among the competition. Make it a point to research these and see if they are of any use to your organization. One of my clients regularly sits in on these meetings and according to him "everyone now wears the same color shirt. The lines are so blurred between us, that there is very little we don't know about each other."

We have allowed for innovative and creative ideas that may sound crazy at the time.

It is often the "crazy" ideas that reap the greatest rewards. (For more on this topic see *Blue Ocean Strategy* by W. Chan Kim and Renee Mauborgne). Based on the study of 150 strategic moves spanning a hundred years and thirty industries, the authors argue that leading companies will not succeed by fighting over increasingly shrinking market space with tiny, incremental improvements, but instead must make powerful leaps in value by virtue of creating "blue oceans" of uncontested market space ripe for growth. As an example, when Ted Turner proposed a 24-hour news channel (CNN) they told him he was crazy. The same was said of Bill Gates when he suggested everyone could have a computer on their desk, or when Ivan

Seidenberg decided to invest $23,000,000,000 over ten years in fiber optic cable for Verizon. An organizational culture that allows for crazy ideas is a culture that will benefit from those very same ideas.

We shut down any negativity around creative thought.

Equally as important as a culture that promotes innovation and creativity, is the willingness to hold those who shut it down or behave negatively towards it, accountable. This can be difficult, especially when the naysayers are in senior or decision-making positions.

Allowing your teams to both succeed *and* fail is critical, as long as you allow them the freedom to try. Knowing when (and if) to step in is a key leadership skill, and one that should be employed judiciously. Psychological research shows that the human brain evolved to react much more strongly to negative experiences than positive ones. This mechanism essentially keeps us safe from danger. In the business environment, this is referred to as the negativity bias. Negativity can hurt organizational productivity AND innovation. In the human brain, about two-thirds of the amygdala (the part responsible for motivation and emotion) is designed to focus on negativity. An example of this is found in economic studies that show people are more likely to make both financial and career decisions based on avoiding the bad versus achieving good. This type of thinking is prevalent in many industries. Coined "risk aversion," it can stifle creativity. System improvement team leaders must be keenly aware of this negativity bias and work to ensure that team member's emotions and perceptions are managed along with the idea flow.

We have documented our brainstorming efforts.

Documentation of the brainstorming outcome is especially important in order to avoid many of the pitfalls of unsuccessful brainstorming efforts, such as bias and groupthink. It also allows fresh eyes and ideas to review past ideas for relevance or application to other systems or identified bottlenecks. I have mentioned the use of online white boards as a way to keep records of your progress. These can be very effective and inexpensive. On occasion, the team should go back over and review previous ideas in the context of any new observations or findings. In addition, this is a simple and timely way to bring new team members up to speed quickly.

Our ideas will increase the capacity of our identified bottlenecks and positively impact the performance of our system.

One surefire way to derail both meetings and brainstorming sessions (on any topic) is to veer off-course and run down every imaginable rabbit hole. While outside-the-box thinking and creativity are important, it is equally important to stay focused on those ideas with the greatest potential to increase the capacity of the identified bottleneck, and ultimately improve the business goals of the organization. It is important to occasionally perform a gut-check against the ideas being generated and to ensure that they are in alignment. It is ultimately the responsibility of the system improvement team leader to circle back to these questions at regular intervals.

Our brainstorming ideas are aligned with the business goals of our organization.

Finally, while reviewing and assessing the output of your brainstorming sessions it is vital to make sure those ideas you intend to pursue are in alignment with these very same goals. And remember, it is not just a matter of knowing your expected Return on Investment. The team must consider each and every second- and third-level effect as well. You must understand all impacts to the business goals, to the organization, to the workforce, to the competition, and to your clients.

Finally, while reviewing and assessing the output of your brainstorming sessions it is vital to make sure those ideas you intend to pursue are in alignment with these very same goals. And remember, it is not just a matter of knowing your expected Return on Investment. The team must consider each and every second- and third-level effect as well. You must understand all impacts to the business goals, to the organization, to the workforce, to the competition, and to your clients.

THE LEGO Case Study According to Step 6:
Brainstorm

While Ashcroft does not specifically describe the brainstorming process used by LEGO during its transition, according to Jonathan Ringen in his February 2015 *Fast Company* article, "How LEGO Became the Apple of Toys," it is readily apparent that the brainstorming process is inherent in the culture of the organization. As part of the turnaround, Ringen states that Knudstorp accomplished the turnaround in part by performing research including deep ethnographic studies on how kids around the world really play. Knudstorp later used this research and brainstorm process to create LEGO'S Future Lab, the toy giant's secretive and highly innovative R+D team, who hold extensive brainstorm sessions and field trips that include their idea of the Right Team: industrial designers, interaction designers, programmers, ethnographic researchers, marketers and master builders. The purpose of these sessions is simple—"generate bigger, deeper, more awesome ideas."

Step 6	BRAINSTORM FORM

Our team and our leader hold us accountable to the following rules:

BRAINSTORM GROUND RULES

	✓
Our system improvement team has developed a culture that promotes innovation, ideas and brainstorming.	
Our team avoids bias.	
Our team avoids groupthink.	
We understand that avoiding bias and groupthink will increase our team's innovation.	
We have considered examples of benchmarking and best practices from both inside and outside our organization.	
We have allowed for innovative and creative ideas that may sound crazy at the time	
We shut down any negativity around creative thought.	
We have documented our brainstorming efforts.	
Our ideas will increase the capacity of our identified bottlenecks and positively impact the performance of our system.	
Our brainstorming ideas are aligned with the business goals of our organization.	
I am not in love with the idea because it is my idea.	
We do not like the idea because we finally decided on an idea, any idea.	
We did not decide on this idea because the loudest person in the room championed it.	
We did not pick this idea because it was successful in the past.	
We did not pick this idea because the owner of the idea has had success in the past.	
We did not pick this idea based on unsubstantiated data, numbers or metrics.	
We did not pick this idea because it will be the cheapest to implement.	
We did not pick this idea because we know management will approve it.	
We get this idea because it was the best idea.	
We have challenged where our data comes from.	
We have challenged whether our metrics are correct.	
We have challenged whether our proposed changes are in alignment with the business goals of the organization and will increase the capacity of our bottleneck.	
We do not assume our questions are correct, and we have asked those questions that identify the correct root causes.	
We do not assume our answers are correct, and we have consensus within our team and from the appropriate stakeholders that these are the correct answers.	

Brainstorm summary can be found here: ▶
(Real Time board, attachment, file name, etc.)

Step 7:
Select Optimal Solution(s)
for Improvement

"The man who removes a mountain begins
by carrying away small stones."

—Chinese Proverb

*Ensure the best recommendations for system change are selected based
upon thorough cost-benefit analysis, peer and stakeholder review.*

Now that you have completed the brainstorming process, the task of
selecting only ONE solution for implementation starts. Step 7
includes a series of important questions designed to determine
whether or not you have chosen the most objective optimal solu-
tion(s) for improvement to your system. Those solutions that have
been selected should be analytically and quantitatively assessed, and
the "math" needs to be done to ensure that their potential impacts
have positive outcomes for the business.

In every case, those solutions that are ultimately selected need to
be tied to the financial impacts to the organization. Often, ideas for
improvement within organizations are selected and approved for
implementation without any true cost-benefit analysis being performed. When they are selected because a favorite employee has been
championing their value, the appearance (without quantitative
back-up) of a positive outcome, or outside pressure from management, clients, or stakeholders, the optimal solutions for improvement
are *only* those solutions that have passed the cost-benefits sniff test.

STEP 7—IN THE REAL WORLD

The purpose of Step 7 is to provide confidence that you have "done the math" to ensure that the solution(s) to removing the process bottleneck supports your goal of improving the business goals of your organization. In other words, not every idea is the best idea (even if it has the "wow" factor and seems like the best idea).

Step 7 is the analysis of the idea, the part where you put the proverbial pen-to-paper and empirically assess the cost-benefit ratio of your prioritized solutions. So not only do you need to assess the performance impacts of your solutions, but the actual costs (in dollars). For Client A, the structural productivity group performed this analysis across their top ideas, and landed on the top two. The root cause of significant bottlenecks in the structural process had been identified as the varied elevations within the fabrication facility. These variations posed significant challenges to craft in maintaining fabrication processes as level as possible, as well as cost significant dollars in set-up equipment and man-hours across projects.

The team decided to tackle this problem by evaluating several possible set-up styles:

- Existing
- Top hat
- Engineered
- Hydraulic
- Other

Upon performing a detailed cost-benefit analysis, it found that two types of set-ups:

- ○ Fixed for primary steel
- ○ Adjustable set-ups

had the greatest Return On Investment (ROI) of all possible solutions. These two set-ups would now improve productivity and thus enable the crew to frame out faster. In the analysis, the structural team made sure that this increased productivity of fabrication did not ultimately increase inventory or operating expense, nor did it negatively impact Safety or Quality (the other two business goals).

Once this set-up solution was implemented and tested, the team went after the second bottleneck: primary steel.

The team recognized that primary steel was a constraint to secondary steel, and implemented a work plan that enabled the crew to do two types of work simultaneously, thus improving efficiency.

As can be seen from the brief overview provided here, the brainstorming ideas that resulted in these solutions had a significant positive impact on Client A operations. Throughput was increased, and unit-rates decreased, both of which allowed Client A to improve overall productivity, continue to bid competitively, and ultimately assist its clients in reaching project completion faster.

The purpose of a cost-benefit analysis is to determine whether or not the system improvement is worthwhile to the organization. The analysis estimates the total overall equivalent money value of both the benefits and the costs to the organization in a holistic manner. The concept of cost-benefit originated with French engineer Jules Dupuit in 1848, and was later formalized by British economist Alfred Marshall. Later, the U.S. Army Corps of Engineers created a systematic method to determine the value of waterway projects under the Federal Navigation Act of 1936. The process is commonly used today in most businesses.

One of the most important tenets of a cost-benefit analysis is to find a common unit of measurement. For the purposes of the 9 Steps, this common unit of measurement is always dollars ($). Keep in mind that when evaluating the bottom-line ($), if you have other business goals identified in Step 3 (Identify the Goal), that these units of measurement must also be evaluated. And ultimately, none of the business goals can be negatively impacted (whether $, safety: # of incidents, quality: # errors, etc.). During this step it will be essential to monetize the impacts to the other identified business goals, in order to calculate an overall dollar impact of the entire system change. In other words, all costs and benefits of your one system improvement/change must be measured in terms of their equivalent money value. That also means that any ancillary benefits must be quantified in dollar values.

Not only do you need to express the costs and benefits in dollar values, but in units of time. The reason for this is simple: it takes into account the cost of inflation as well as the value of earning interest on dollars not invested now, and particularly for those changes that may not realize their ROI for several years, this can become important. The cost-benefit analysis also needs to reflect the value of time saved. The question becomes how to measure the dollar value of that time saved. This value should not simply reflect what the members of the system improvement team, or even those who work within the system, think the time should be worth. But it should reflect the value of time in the *tradeoff* between money and time. For example, if people have a choice of parking at an airport for $50 or parking further away and spending five minutes more walking across a bridge to the airport, and they always choose to spend the money and save the time, they have calculated that their time is worth more than $10 per minute. But if they chose each option equally, this means they think the value of their time would be exactly $10 per minute.

In some situations, implementing one optimal system improvement may cause negative impacts to other business goals (quality for example), but the OVERALL impact is positive. As such, in some situations your system improvements may cause an overall increase in $ profit, but negatively impact other business goals. Other than with regard to Safety goals (I am loathe to calculate the dollar value of a human life) this can be acceptable and should be taken into your overall cost-benefit calculations. This is yet another reason why the monetization of all business goals and impacts, as well as performing the cost-benefit analysis becomes so critical to the 9 Step process.

The checklist on page 138 is designed to guide you through the cost-benefit process:

We have "done the math" to prioritize the outputs of our brainstorming, and have shown that these will have the greatest impact on our business goals in the Cost-Benefit Checklist)

As stated in the opening of this section, each potential solution needs to pass the empirical cost-benefit test to determine its potential for actual value to the business goals of the organization. The Cost-Benefit Checklist provides a brief overview of those requirements to perform, at a minimum, a financial analysis of any potential changes to the system.

STEP 7 CHECKLIST

- We have "done the math" to prioritize the outputs of our brainstorming, and have shown that these will have the greatest impact on our business goals. (See Cost-Benefit Checklist.)

- We have discussed our prioritized recommendations for change with a Peer Review group and have their buy-in.

- We have management buy-in to implement these changes.

- We have analyzed the potential impact of these proposed changes to our system and to our organization as a whole.

- In selecting these recommendations, we have conducted a thorough cost-benefit analysis prior to prioritization. (See Cost-Benefit Checklist.)

- We have double-checked that any changes we recommend will have the highest positive impact to the business goals of our organization.

- We have used the correct tools and methodology to select our solutions (RCA, time studies, research).

- We will provide a proof of concept and proof of concept budget if required.

As can be seen from the Cost-Benefit Checklist, each of the included checklist items requires the quantification of any costs or savings to both the system and the organization as a whole in actual dollars and on an annualized basis. In order to make sound business decisions, it is essential to always understand any Return-on-Investment (ROI) for capital expenditures, as well as all fully-loaded costs to the system. The simplest way to quantify these costs and maintain consistency in using the 9 Steps model, is to tie dollar amounts to the same cost categories as determined in the Theory of Constraints language:

- **Throughput** = $ profit

- **Inventory** = $ cost for facilities, equipment, obsolete items, raw materials, work-in-progress, finished goods

- **Operating Expense** = $ cost direct labor, utilities, consumable supplies, depreciation of assets

After categorizing total costs across each of these categories, positive and negative financial impacts across each category can be calculated (within identified system boundaries only). It is important to not only quantify system impacts in dollar amounts, but to ensure any ongoing system performance metrics are directly related to these financial measures.

The Cost-Benefit Checklist provides clear direction on which financial impacts to take into consideration. It is important to delineate between actual costs and potential costs (for example, you may choose to calculate projected costs and benefits prior to implementing any proposed system changes, and then comparing these projections to calculated actuals after observing changes to the system). Once again, using the terminology of the Theory of Constraints can be helpful, as it is important to measure **only** those cost-benefit impacts within the boundaries of your identified system in Step 1.

The fifth item of the Cost-Benefit Checklist will require you to incorporate not only the costs/benefits in dollars associated within the boundaries of your identified system, but also upstream and downstream financial impacts.

Finally, when performing this financial analysis, it is important to make sure that the **organizational and system** performance metrics are directly tied to the financial impacts. For example, it is pointless to measure an amount of work produced in man-hours, feet, parts, inches, weld rate, units, and so forth if these metrics are not directly tied to the dollars required to produce them. Producing work for work's sake is not productive. Producing work for profit's sake is the purpose behind these kinds of business decisions.

Cost-Benefit Checklist

- We have identified the overall benefits of this improvement in a dollar amount.

- We have quantified the costs of any initial investments in a dollar amount.

- We have quantified the cost savings of our proposed change in dollars/year.

- We have quantified the cost-benefit in average dollars/year.

- We have quantified the sum total of financial costs and benefits across the entire system.

- We are properly accounting for all positive and negative financial impacts to our system.

- We have properly tied any impacts to any performance metrics within our system to the financial impacts.

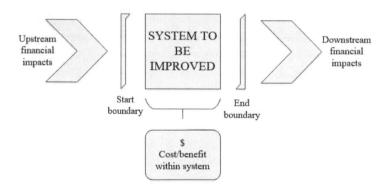

Upstream and Downstream Boundaries

An example of "doing the math" can be seen in what team Alpha accomplishes.

System improvement team Alpha has determined it needs to improve the throughput of a sub-assembly facility. The team has completed Steps 1 through 6, and during the course of their Step 6 Brainstorming has narrowed down the best ideas to three options to improve the facility throughput (in this case its throughput is defined as completing the sub-assemblies just-in-time for delivery to final assembly). This ability to deliver just-in-time significantly reduces inventory costs and solves their problem as the overall bottleneck in the entire assembly operation. Team Alpha has also defined safety and quality as two additional business goals. The metrics include:

○ **Safety:** # incidents

○ **Quality:** % sub-assembly rework errors

○ **Throughput:** % sub-assemblies completed just-in-time

In the brainstorming step, the team has defined the following two system changes as potential solutions:

○ **Solution 1:** Replace a portion of manual assembly with an automated process (robotics).

○ **Solution 2:** Move the sub-assembly portion into the final assembly building (several miles away).

○ **Solution 3:** Do one or the other as the new robotics machine will not fit in the final assembly building.

Since both of these solutions are front-end costly, the cost-benefit analysis is very important. Let's walk through how to prioritize among them (in simplified summary fashion as your analyses should be detailed and thorough). This overly-simplified example is provided to demonstrate the thought process only—and a much more thorough analysis is provided further in this chapter:

Solution 1—Robotics

Inventory $ Impacts (annualized)

> Cost of robotics system: $500,000 *cost (one time)*
>
> Reduction in material waste (less waste automated vs manual): $50,000 saving

Reduced floor space (need to move raw material storage in order to find space for new robotics machine) with increased labor travel time from new storage space at end of facility to assembly position = 10 additional minutes per week/operator = 520 hours/year @ $40.86/hr. = $21,247 *cost*

Operating expense $ Impacts (annualized)

> Reduction in labor costs (two operators at fully-burdened annualized cost of $85,000 each): $170,000 *saving*
>
> Increased utility (electrical) consumption with new robotics: $25,000 *cost*
>
> Depreciation of new robotics machine: $30,000 *cost*
>
> Increased cost of training on new robotic machine: $25,000 *cost*
>
> O&M on new robotics machine: $15,000 *cost*

Throughput $ impacts (annualized)

> Reduced delay of delivery of sub-assembly to final assembly (cut delivery time in half, increase customer response time) $200,000 *saving*

Safety $ Impacts (annualized)

> Reduced hand injuries with automated vs manual assembly: $25,000 *saving*

Quality $ Impacts (annualized)

Decreased % rework due to operator error: $50,000 *savings*

Total Costs

Year 1: $616,247

Year 2 forward: $116,247

Total Savings:

Year 1 forward: $495,000

Calculating a 3 year Return on Investment (ROI) would show:

Year 1: $121,000 cost

Year 2: $378,753 saving

Year 3: $378,753 saving

So that in Year 2 the company would continue to save money with the change to robotics.

Solution 2—Move to Final Assembly Building

Inventory $ Impacts (annualized)

Cost of electrical upgrade in final assembly building (one time): $80,000 *cost*

Utilize floor space in existing sub-assembly for warehouse —eliminate cost of warehouse building: $120,000 *saving*

Operating expense $ Impacts (annualized)

One time moving cost: $100,000 *cost*

Throughput $ impacts (annualized)

Reduced delay of delivery of sub-assembly to final assembly (cut delivery time by 25%, increase customer response time) $100,000 *saving*

Safety $ Impacts (annualized)

Increased risk of safety incidents due to tight working quarters in final assembly building: $75,000 *cost*

Quality $ Impacts (annualized)

No impacts determined

Total Costs

Year 1: $255,000

Year 2 forward: $75,000

Total Savings:

Year 1 forward: $220,000

Calculating a 3 year Return on Investment (ROI) would show:

○ Year 1: $35,000 cost

○ Year 2: $145,000 saving

○ Year 3: $145,000 saving

So that in Year 2 the company would continue to save money with the move to the final assembly building.

As can be seen from this analysis, the company would need to determine if it wanted to commit to a $500,000 capital expenditure on top of the increased operating cost in year 1, but it would also save significant dollars in subsequent years (more than with Solution 2). In this case, moving to the final assembly building would prevent the company from converting to robotics as the machine will not fit in that building, so the decision has significant long-term impacts.

A more detailed and thorough analysis is provided at www.Paradyneconsulting.com/book/forms in Appendix D.

We have discussed our prioritized recommendations for change with a Peer Review group and have their buy-in.

The purpose of a Peer Review is to provide feedback on any proposed changes or recommendations and to gain perspective on past experience and knowledge prior to execution. The Peer Review team should serve as a check-and-balance that mitigates the risk of repeating past difficult mistakes. This collaborative effort is an important validation step that should reduce risk, validate any expenditures and perform an organizational "gut check" on the direction of the proposed changes to the system.

This Peer Review is also a mechanism by which you perform a third-eye review of your cost–benefit analysis and your math. This group will thoroughly dissect your analysis and challenge any and all assumptions. Especially when you are proposing a significant capital expenditure, your Peer review team will need to be on board. Don't be surprised if your idea is met with resistance, particularly if it includes a large dollar amount at the front-end. Frequently, big ideas have big dollar amounts associated with them, and managers who are risk averse may shoot down the idea before it gets off the ground.

I have seen this happen on many occasions. In one instance, a client had a huge rework problem due to sand getting into its paint. The company was located in a region of the country where wind was a constant aggravation. The wind caused fine particles of grit to contaminate the final product especially during certain seasons, and no matter what the company attempted, the grit always won. Finally, one of the project managers put together a cost-benefit analysis for a state-of-the-art indoor paint facility which guaranteed no paint contamination. The ROI showed break-even in as little as four years, with the company realizing savings of $7M, $15M and $24M in each subsequent year. The problem? The up-front capital investment was $30M and not one senior manager was willing to get behind that hefty sum. Their culture was so risk averse that the very notion of exhausting cash reserves was too dangerous to even contemplate. To this day, the client continues to lose money every time the wind kicks up.

We have management buy-in to implement these changes.

In the best scenario, the Peer Review team includes the appropriate managers and decision-makers in attendance in order to efficiently and effectively expedite approval for any changes that require dollars, people, equipment or time. If the system improvement idea is costly, it may be a good idea to propose a scaled-down test version, or otherwise implement the changes in increments. It is important for the system improvement team to consider the temperament and reaction of management to whatever ideas are proposed, and whether or not they will be open to the idea at all. It is always a good idea to communicate often and early with final decision-makers in the event that buy-in will require time. There is nothing more frustrating than sitting on an excellent idea for improvement months on end waiting for approval. Involve your management early in the process so executives are part of the dialogue, start gaining buy-in as soon as you can, and if capital will be required, perform your due diligence to ensure funds are actually available.

We have analyzed the potential impact of these proposed changes to our system and to our organization as a whole.

As part of the Peer Review process, both the team suggesting any changes to the system, as well as the Peer Review team, should be discussing not only the impacts (both financially and organizationally) to the system, but to the organization as a whole. In some cases, changes may involve significant impacts to roles and responsibilities, operations or the "old way" of performing work within the system.

Use your cost-benefit and ROI tools to explain the math behind the idea and the potential positive financial impacts, but also make sure to cover these important cultural changes as part of any discussions.

These types of shocks to the culture of an organization can have significant repercussions, and should be understood in their entirety when approving changes to any component of the organizational system. When system improvements are substantial, they can alter the organization's culture and the reactions of the employees can be startling. Changing an organization's culture is one of the most difficult challenges any leader or team can face, primarily because large-scale changes impact the company's goals, people's roles and responsibilities, channels of communication, individual attitudes and even the vision and future of the company. That is the driving force behind the difficulty of change, because even if a system improvement is worthwhile or exciting at first, the organizational culture will eventually suck both the team and the employees back into the "old way of doing things" vortex.

Without devoting an entire chapter to cultural change, it is important that the team implementing the system improvements understand that it will need to use a series of important tools to implement the changes in order to make them *stick*. There is a substantial amount of literature on this subject, but in essence force and power will not work. An organization will adapt to a new way of doing things if the management team provides a clear vision and story of the new process or system, and communicates its benefits to every employee affected. It is crucial the team leader and any champions of the system improvements discuss these cultural impacts and employee reactions prior to implementing any solutions. I have seen instances where perfectly well-thought out improvements (complete with detailed cost-benefit analyses) have fallen flat due to cultural resistance. A company's culture and employees can be a powerful force to be reckoned with, and I highly recommend that system improvement teams do not underestimate their influence.

Steve Denning in *The Leader's Guide to Radical Management: Reinventing the Workplace for the 21st Century* identifies this process very succinctly:

Do come with a clear vision of where you want the organization to go and promulgate that vision rapidly and forcefully with leadership storytelling.

Do identify the core stakeholders of the new vision and drive the organization to be continuously and systematically responsive to those stakeholders.

Do define the role of managers as enablers of self-organizing teams and draw on the full capabilities of the talented staff.

Do quickly develop and put in place new systems and processes that support and reinforce this vision of the future.

Do introduce and consistently reinforce the values of radical transparency and continuous improvement.

Do communicate horizontally in conversations and stories, not through top-down commands.

Don't start by reorganizing. First clarify the vision and put in place the management roles and systems that will reinforce the vision.

Don't parachute in a new team of top managers. Work with the existing managers and draw on people who share your vision.

In selecting these recommendations, we have conducted a thorough cost-benefit analysis prior to prioritization. (see the Cost-Benefit Checklist)

It is recommended that the team present thorough ROI and cost-benefit calculations as part of both the prioritization effort and presentation to the Peer Review team. Many eyes and brains should assess these calculations for their accuracy, applicability and impacts to the system and organization.

Keep in mind that the impact of a project is the difference between what the system would be like both with, and without, the changes. Therefore, your analysis must estimate not only what the system should be like with the change, but also without. In other words, the alternative (not doing the change) must be explicitly specified and considered in the overall evaluation. On occasion, the impact of a system change or improvement can be measured in several ways. For example, if an improved system reduces time to production and the risk of injury to operators, then the value to the organization will be enhanced. This increase in value to the organization is a good way to measure the success of the project, but if the increased value of the company is included in the cost-benefit, then you are double-counting.

The equivalent money measurement is the best way to measure if your project or change is worthwhile. Always take into account things like inflation, depreciation, and other easily overlooked effects.

We have double-checked that any changes we recommend will have the highest positive impact to the business goals of our organization.

The selection of the optimal solution(s) must include a quantitative analysis of any impacts to the business goals of the organization. For example, if the change to the system results in higher sales revenue—it may be seen as a positive impact to the system. However, if the business goal of the organization is profit, and this new revenue stream cannot quantitatively be shown to be profitable, then it is not an optimal solution. As previously stated in the above examples, always count those impacts (in equivalent dollars) to your other business goals. It can be easy to get caught up in the *newness* of a concept or change and forget to double-back and review the impact on each and every business goal that was identified at the beginning of the 9 Steps.

We have used the correct tools and methodology to select our solutions (RCA, time studies, research).

As can be seen throughout Step 7, empirical and objective data is critical to the unbiased selection of the most sound, innovative and business goal-oriented solutions. There are many analytical tools at your disposal that can be used to select solutions. Time studies, root cause analysis (RCA), Kaizen, are just a few. Step 4 of the 9 Steps identifies these tools in detail (as does Appendix C). To review: Fishbone Diagram, Kaizen, DMAIC, Root Cause Analyses (RCA), Job Hazard Analyses (JHA) and others, all of which can be used to observe current systems. No matter what tools you use, the purpose remains the same: to properly, methodically, analytically and systemically observe and document your system in a way that can be reproduced and analyzed quantitatively and objectively by others.

The reason for using analytical tools is simple: the observer must remove any personal or organizational bias from the results; otherwise the results are false. If your system is a business or process system (non-production or operations) the methodology remains of the same, while the system specifics may differ. Do not assume you can skip this step if you work within an internal department and your "operations" are not directly tied to a project or operations process. It is also important that you go back through your system improvement process and double-check that you have indeed used the right tools and methodology to select your final solutions for implementation and that the idea you are implementing has not bypassed the important precursor steps.

Select those tools that are most applicable to your operation, and can provide you with the hard data necessary to make selections. Any system that produces work (whether a product or a service) can be objectively analyzed, and utilizing the proper methodology is key to truly understanding impacts within the system. If you or those on your team are not experts in utilizing these tools, hire someone who is. The outcomes may radically alter your view of your current work processes.

We will provide a proof of concept and proof of concept budget if required.

In some cases it may be essential to model, simulate or prototype your system improvements as actual changes to the system may be too costly. A proof of concept is simply a tool to verify that your system improvement idea is feasible. Typically, a proof of concept is a scaled-down, less costly version of your idea.

Be prepared to present the fully-scaled version on paper. Make sure the system improvement team understands how to integrate the larger version and vets all potential impacts. Make sure your math takes into account all fully-burdened costs and identifies any challenges to implementation. Identify all required resources, facilities, equipment, safety and quality impacts.

Depending upon your industry, proof of concept could have different definitions for the following:

Engineering and Technology:

A rough prototype of a novel idea is constructed as a working concept. Patents often require demonstration of functionality prior to filing. Ideas are scaled down to reduce implementation costs while demonstrating feasibility.

Software Development:

In software development there are several definitions:

○ A steel thread is technical proof of concept that touches all of the technologies in a solution.

○ Proof of technology aims to determine the solution to some technical problem (such as how two systems might integrate) or to demonstrate that a given configuration can achieve a certain throughput.

○ A pilot project refers to an initial roll-out of a system into production, targeting a limited scope of the intended final solution. The purpose of a pilot project is to test, often in a production environment.

Sales or Service:

In the field of sales or in service-related industries, a vendor may allow a prospective customer to trial a product. This use of proof-of-concept helps to establish viability, to isolate technical issues, and to suggest overall direction, as well as providing feedback for budgeting and other forms of internal decision-making processes.

No matter your industry, the idea is relatively straightforward: simply provide viable proof that your idea will work prior to spending large dollars on its purchase and implementation. Most managers appreciate this type of cost-effective thinking, and it is always a good idea to mitigate financial risk.

The LEGO Case Study According to Step 7:
Optimal Solutions

In the LEGO case study, it became readily obvious to both Knudstorp and Oresen that, not only were the financial metrics incorrect, but the decision-making behind the financial strategy was flawed. Together, they believed the optimal solution(s) for stemming the losses revolved around a succinct and clear series of events designed to manage the business for cash, rather than sales growth. Their solutions? Sell off the theme parks, slow retail expansion, reduce the product offerings and cut 1,000 employees from the work force. "Back to basics" was the new mantra for LEGO, and according to the Knudstorp, "the successful implementation of these initiatives was crucial for LEGO Company to ensure profitable growth, and that the same time, uphold its strong, global brand position among families with children."

Step 7	OPTIMAL SOLUTION(S) FORM

Summary of Step 6 Brainstorm Outputs:

▶

The following brainstorm ideas have the most value to the business goals based on the analysis below:

Productivity/profit:	▶
	▶
Quality:	▶
	▶
Safety:	▶
	▶

Financial Impacts:

Cost-Benefit Analysis	Brainstorm 1	Brainstorm 2	Brainstorm 3
$ cost any initial investments/year			
$ cost saving of proposed changes ($/year)			
If capital investment—term of payback (years)			
System performance metrics to be utilized (must be tied to cost-benefit above):			

Step 7 cont'd	OPTIMAL SOLUTION(S) FORM

	Pre-Proof of Concept	Post Proof of Concept
Prioritized List of Optimal Solution(s):	1.	1.
	2.	2.
	3.	3.

We will present our findings to the following Peer Review/Management group for approval:

Name	Position	Email	Phone

Proof of Concept Budget:_____

Proof of Concept Completion Date:_____

Proof of Concept Owner:_____

Summary of Proof of Concept Results:

▶ Solutions Approved By:	▶ Solutions Approved By:

Signature	Date	Signature	Date

Step 8:
Implement One Change at a Time

"Never doubt that a small group of thoughtful, committed
citizens can change the world.
Indeed, it is the only thing that ever has."

—MARGARET MEAD
Coming of Age in Samoa

*Implement any proposed change independently of any other changes to
ensure any measured impacts are the result of this change alone.*

Step 8 is straightforward in that it requires planned and systematic
implementation of any changes to the system. It is virtually impossible to quantify the true impacts to, and within, a system without clear
and defined boundaries. The implementation of multiple solutions or
approaches only blurs the issue, and makes the analytical portion
practically impossible, as it becomes unclear which change actually
positively or negatively impacted the system as a whole.

The system improvement team should not underestimate the organizational response to ANY proposed changes. Change management
is an art in and of itself and there are many books and articles on this
subject. For the purposes of this chapter we will discuss change management as part of the 9 Step process and utilize an elegant model proposed by Harold L. Sirkin, Perry Keenan and Alan Jackson in the
October 2005 *Harvard Business Review* article "The Hard Side of
Change Management."

Making improvements to your system (or any changes for that
matter) is a process, not an event. Achieving a shift in culture is not
an easy task, and implementing your improvements one change at a

time can be daunting. Just because you announce your idea or hold a meeting does not mean everyone will automatically buy in. The system improvement team must consider the transition of the existing process and people to the new way of doing things. Both your organization and the employees involved will be impacted, and as a team, you must manage both.

The system improvement team leader along with those on the team must work together to understand the impacts of any changes at the individual level in order for the change to be both successful and to improve your business performance. The idea is to be aware of their reactions and provide both the information and tools necessary to accept and implement the new changes. All the people could have different reactions to the proposed new system, depending upon how much impact it has on their roles and responsibilities. If, for example, a new process eliminates one or more positions, it is critical that the leader and team find ways to communicate this in a positive manner and work together with those individuals impacted to ensure movement to another position or otherwise support their transition. Without this support, the likelihood of rumors and gossip run high, and the team will face an uphill battle to implement any of their ideas successfully.

When managing change at the organizational level, watch for those key indicators that will signal resistance or dismissal. Make sure to clearly communicate the need for, the vision of, and the strategy and intended outcomes of implementation early and often. The team needs to also identify any training or resources needed by current process users to adapt to the new system improvement. The communication plan needs to explain:

- Why the current system needs improvement
- Details about how and why the final solution was selected
- Clear milestones and deliverables for the implementation
- The need to provide an open forum for questions

The training should include:

- ○ Clear identification of the new skills required
- ○ A timeline for training and implementation
- ○ Transition coaching into new roles

Additionally, the system improvement team will need to track whether or not the change to the system has been successful or not. This needs to be accomplished along two fronts: performance metrics (impacts to your business goals) and system improvement project success (is it sustainable and part of your ongoing organizational culture). Sirkin, Keenan, and Jackson offer a simple model to help monitor progress and this model is outlined below.*

Defined as "hard factors" the authors describe how when attempting to incorporate new system improvements successfully into existing companies, the recent trend among professionals has been to focus on "soft issues," such as "culture, leadership, and motivation" and to consider the role that these will play in a program's long-term success. This more general approach, however, neglects to consider the extremely important role which "hard factors" play in determining whether or not a system improvement will ultimately be successful. Hard factors are defined by their ability to be measured directly or indirectly by companies, have importance which can be readily explained both in and beyond the company, and can be swiftly swayed by the company. A solution to this deficiency is the DICE method* outlined by the authors which offers a reliable and accurate measurement of how likely it is that a change to your system will succeed in specific situations depending on the hard factors at play.

The DICE program identifies four specific hard factors which each have direct impact upon the overall outcome of implementing a change to your system. They are project duration, performance integrity, commitment of both senior executives and staff, and additional employee effort which will be required by the planned implementation. These are factors which can be loaded to better ensure the success of implementing change or system improvements. More specific exploration of these four factors will provide a clearer understanding of their broader function in the DICE model and how they can be influenced in order to ensure system improvement success.

The definition of the first factor, which is the duration of the system improvement, differs slightly depending on whether or not the project is relatively long or short. If the project is long, duration should be defined as the amount of time which elapses between milestone assessments built into the program; if the project's length is relatively short, duration should be measured as the timespan of the entire program. The existing assumption about projects in business today is that a longer program will more likely fail than a shorter one, since companies fear that a longer initiative means a loss of interest and momentum, and ultimately, project failure. However, recent research indicates that, in fact, longer programs, when reviewed frequently, have a greater success rate than shorter programs. If a project is reviewed effectively over its entire duration, therefore, its chances of success are significantly increased.

The DICE approach offers specific suggestions for proper reviewing procedures to maximize chances of program success. It suggests that so-called transformation projects ought to be reviewed at least twice a month since the chances of problems arising with a program are substantially increased when the time between reviews exceeds eight weeks at a time. It specifies that more intricate projects should be reviewed at least once every two weeks and more straightforward ones can survive with reviews perhaps once every six to eight weeks at a time. Reviews can be scheduled more frequently if executives deem them necessary to project success. In general, milestone reviews are most effectively scheduled so as to measure major steps or achievements in the program, thus giving executives the greatest chance of catching problems with the program. Establishing formal reviews on a schedule derived from project duration as suggested by DICE provides company leaders an effective method of ensuring program success. (See Step 9 for a further discussion on how to incorporate this review into your Productivity Review Team.)

Besides duration, performance integrity plays an important role in determining whether or not a specific program will succeed. Integrity is defined as the reliance of companies on their employees to ensure that system improvements get incorporated successfully. The DICE method suggests that company executives must take a proactive role in assembling the project team by using a comprehensive process to select the best employees for the job, making the criteria for each team position readily available to employees, and by seeking the best in their company for every specific task available. (This aligns directly with Step 2: Put the Right Team Together.) They must be sure to interview the candidates before assigning them to the available positions as well as assign specific dates and times that the employees on the project team will devote to completing the project, in addition to their regular duties. Completing these steps will ensure that the project team selected is the best the company has to offer and will be up to the task of successfully implementing the selected optimal solutions for system improvement.

Commitment of executives and affected employees to system improvement is another important factor in determining whether or not a program will succeed in a company. Firstly, DICE suggests that it is absolutely essential to have a large number of senior managers on board; doing so makes it more likely that others will be more inclined to back the effort to implement the new program. Secondly, the employees who must deal with the new program's structures on a regular basis must support the project since they are the ones who will have to interact with it the most and therefore are the most affected by whatever changes the program will implement. If they do not support the program, they will be less likely to follow its requirements, undermining the program in an extremely significant way. Ensuring the commitment and support of these important employees better helps ensure that the program will be successful. This concept aligns directly with Steps 3–7 of the 9 Steps.

Finally, effort, or the additional workload that the implementation of such a program will place on existing employees of a company, can also have a major impact on program success. Employees of a company are already extremely busy without the additional tasks added by implementing any system improvements, and the DICE method argues that it is important that the selected system improvement teams calculate the amount of work the new project will add to existing employee workloads. If a workload is expanded by more than 10 percent for any one employee, the program as a whole may be in trouble, as after that point employees become overstretched and will lose enthusiasm.

Companies can relieve this pressure by limiting the amount of tasks that employees essential to the program must perform beyond the program, or by hiring additional help to perform these routine tasks, freeing up the project team until the program is fully in force. Effort, in these ways, can help ensure an introduced system improvements project's long-term success.

The DICE method argues that duration, integrity, commitment (to be measured in two parts: executive commitment as C1 and average worker commitment as C2), and effort must all be factored into a company's plan to introduce a change management program in order to maximize the program's chances of success. These four factors can be measured specifically through the DICE score calculation system, which rates each factor on a scale of 1 to 4 according to established scoring guidelines. Factors which score a 1 will be boons to system improvement success; factors which score a 4 will be detriments. The DICE score can then be calculated by inputting the scores to the equation included in the figure of the DICE model. This calculation can be used as a measure of whether or not the project will likely prove to be successful or not. As indicated in the figure of the Dice Model, scores of 7–14 indicate a program likely destined for success, scores of 14–17 highlight cause for concern for the project's fate, and scores of 17–28 suggest that the project is probably destined for failure.

These scores can provide a highly beneficial framework for use by companies evaluating projects to help determine whether or not their potential system improvement projects should be attempted or continued or if additional steps must be taken to align resources and support to improve the DICE project score. Overall, the DICE method is a simple, yet highly effective measurement tool for companies looking to improve performance, productivity, and profit with a 9 Step approach.

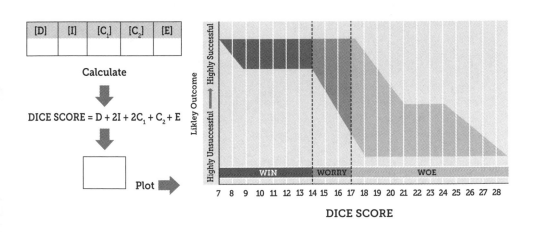

Diagram of the DICE Model

STEP 8 CHECKLIST

- We have implemented only one change that has been approved by all appropriate decision-makers.

- We have identified the correct metrics to track the impacts of this change to our system.

- We have ensured that the metrics we are using to measure change are tied directly to the business goals of the organization.

- We have measured and tracked the changes to our system and tied them directly to our cost-benefit. (Identified in Cost Benefit Checklist)

- We have documented all measured impacts of the changes within our system, both positive and negative.

- We have documented all unintended consequences as a result of our change as well.

- We do not let either failure or success of our changes impact our analysis.

- We have ensured that we completed all elements of our change, and that we have done everything we can to put the change to rest.

The Step 8 Checklist serves as a governing mechanism that ensures not only a focus on one change to the system at a time, but the precise and continuous capture of any data resulting from observations of the impacts of these changes. This data can ultimately be used to evaluate future proposed changes and their impacts as well.

We have implemented only one change that has been approved by all appropriate decision-makers.

As part of the Peer Review process outlined in Step 7, each change should be agreed upon and discussed in its entirety as a stand-alone proposition. Implementation of changes should be done in a systematic, one-by-one manner, with the best ideas implemented first, and their impacts measured and defined before any further changes to the system are made. It is the responsibility of the team leader (as well as the members of the team) to ensure that the ideas do not blur together and become impossible to track. Clear and definitive system change boundaries must be identified at the outset and all appropriate stakeholders need to be bought into that single system improvement.

We have identified the correct metrics to track the impacts of this change to our system.

It cannot be overstated how important the development and tracking of the proper metrics is to the success of improving any system or operation. The old adage of comparing "apples to apples" is critical in this context. There are two sets of metrics that must be tracked:

- The set of performance metrics related to your business goals (profit, safety, quality, etc.) and whether these are ultimately improving with the implementation of the changes to the system.

- Those metrics designed to capture whether the organizational culture is accepting of the system changes (the DICE metrics).

It is recommended that you utilize the DICE model to track whether your system changes have been effective. Although the DICE assessments can be subjective, the model gives your organization an objective framework to decide if the system changes have been effective and sustainable.

I have observed this loss of momentum often, despite how successful the system improvement changes have been on the actual process performance metrics. Without continuous attention, changes within systems are difficult to maintain. In my opinion this is primarily due to lack of attention rather than a loss of desire. Most organizations I work with have the inertia of the old way of doing things swaying the momentum of the new way. People, resources, and time get in the way. It requires diligence and effort to maintain both changes to your system and a shift in culture.

One excellent way to handle this issue is the example of my client who assigned a senior "productivity manager" to combat this loss of momentum and to be the guardian of the new way of doing things. His job is to monitor and track all new 9 Step ideas, make sure the forms are being filled-out properly, hold managers accountable to creating a culture of respect and openness to innovation and trust, and to track and monitor the actual progress and impact to the business goals. Every month the productivity team gets together and reports on each and every system improvement, its status, where they are in the 9 Step process, and the profit, safety, and quality metrics. In one year, this team was able to contribute an additional 1% ($4.2M) to their company's net profit.

We have ensured that the metrics we are using to measure change are tied directly to the business goals of the organization.

This serves as another check-and-balance mechanism designed as a failsafe to make sure the innovation team, the Peer Review group, and the ultimate decision-makers truly understand and can replicate the financial impacts or changes to the business goals of the organization. While the DICE metrics are designed to capture the success of change management, the metrics referred to here are those metrics defined in Step 3 to measure the quantifiable impact on your system. At the end of the day, you need to be able to answer this single important question:

Has this system improvement made more money for my organization?

If the answer is no, then the team must return to the drawing board and select another idea for implementation. It does not matter if the employees are happier, if the managers feel satisfied, if the system *seems* better. You must be able to quantify and measure the equivalent dollar value of your changes and how they impact your bottom line. That is the essence and purpose of the 9 Steps process.

We have measured and tracked the changes to our system and tied them directly to our cost-benefit. (Identified in Cost Benefit Checklist)

Each change must follow a definitive process that includes an analysis in isolation from other impacts. It is important to always go back to the cost-benefit exercise for each and every change and not to skip this step simply because you have completed it for any prior attempts at change. While in the pre-implementation phase of your system improvement, you performed a cost-benefit and *projected* ROI, for this step you must calculate the *actual* ROI. This is also an important step, as often the final results may not mirror the proposed impacts. If the end results are not what was expected (either positively or negatively) the results must be tabulated, published, and reviewed with all relevant stakeholders in every case.

I have seen this step skipped many times. The results can be disastrous. One client had decided to implement a new software system that would migrate three separate functions into one holistic system. They did everything right. The manager and team assigned to the project had clearly identified the need for a system improvement. They selected a top-notch team, that team set clear goals, dissected their current system and defined quantifiable metrics, targeted their pain points (bottlenecks), brainstormed excellent ideas, and landed on the solution that made the most sense to improving efficiency. Their new and improved software integrated all of the parts and pieces of the old system into a single, streamlined model that decreased the number of data entry employees by almost 25 percent, a significant savings in overhead. Additionally, the ROI showed increased efficiency would improve their service throughput by another 30 percent, thus enabling them to process internal documents much faster. I recall the new, custom-programmed system was going to be quite costly up front, but the ROI showed a return after three years and management was convinced this was the right way to go.

So away they went—consultants were brought in, process mapping was completed, and programming began. Well into Year 2 they realized that they needed to incorporate several other elements into the system, and the cost almost doubled. Management forged ahead. At the end of Year 3, the new system was delayed by yet another glitch. Finally, the system was declared ready at the end of Year 4, and all end users were told to go live. By this point just about everyone was culturally dismayed with the entire project. There was little to any buy-in to the value of the new system and many employees simply used spreadsheets instead of the new software. Actual usage was spotty, efficiencies were not fully realized and the project was a costly and monumental failure. Had the team performed this gut-check step and tied back the new costs identified in Year 2, they would have realized that the ROI was no longer feasible and that abandoning the project at that time would have been much less costly. A better approach would have been to go back to the drawing board at that moment and find another solution that would have met the cost-benefit criteria.

We have documented all measured impacts of the changes within our system, both positive and negative.

One of the easiest things to overlook throughout the 9 Steps process is ongoing documentation of all findings, both positive and negative. It can be an arduous and time-consuming process, and many find it easier to skip this step.

An effective tool to document ongoing brainstorming sessions, updated documents, and a chronology of events is RealtimeBoard (www.realtimeboard.com), an online collaborative tool similar to the whiteboards of old, but with an updated, electronic format. Whether you use an electronic version or a simple piece of paper is not important, but documenting your process is. The reason for this is simply for others to be able to duplicate your results as well as research any methodologies you may have used. It is just as important to document your negative results so that future teams do not duplicate them.

In the case of the productivity team mentioned in the previous step, they handle this by setting aside ten minutes in their monthly productivity meetings to discuss "winners" and "losers" and where they are archived (in a Best Practices folder on an internally shared drive).

We have documented all unintended consequences as a result of our change as well.

In many instances, the unintended consequences of a change ultimately provides the answer you are looking for, as opposed to the preconceived answer or solution. Documentation of these (sometimes seemingly insignificant) consequences is vital to the process and can often lead to that heavily sought after "Eureka!" moment.

I have seen many projects take a left turn mid-change. As the implementation progresses, things happen, oftentimes not remotely related to the original intention. It is these very same unintended consequences that often lead to the very best solutions. Watch diligently for these, as they can be game changers.

As an example, one of the system improvement teams I worked with had landed on the idea of building a prototype to prove that a new technology application would solve an internal (and very costly) bottleneck. To buy the new technology and implement it wholesale was determined to be both risky and very expensive. So the team set out to develop a proof of concept prototype for demonstration to the Peer Review team. During the course of building the prototype, one of their own engineers while researching a component for the prototype stumbled across a European company that made another, simpler technology that could replace both the prototype and the need for the larger system altogether. This new idea neatly solved all of their problems in a very simple, elegant, and cost-effective way.

STEP 8—IN THE REAL WORLD

Step 8 requires tremendous discipline. When your team has landed upon what it considers to be the optimal and best solutions, a natural inclination is to run out and try every single one. The problem with that approach is the inability to gauge, document, and replicate any one change, as opposed to a cumulative impact.

The method that the Client A team utilized to ensure they were implementing only one change at a time was to tackle the issues in the sequence of fabrication and assembly. Each idea was analyzed and implemented separately and apart from the others, and only until the impact of each one (set-ups, time on fabrication, secondary steel staging, welders and access) was observed, documented, and understood, was the next solution implemented.

Results were tracked through a dashboard system on a monthly basis, where unit rates, man-hours and dollars were assiduously monitored and evaluated, not only by the structural team, but through an arduous Peer Review process. Team members had to quantitatively and pictorially support their solutions and results and the Peer Review process allowed for challenge and accountability. A Field Operations Report was also created to make sure every change was replicable, and these reports were trained and disseminated to all relevant stakeholders in the operation.

If the unit-rates did not continue to decrease, assumptions were challenged and new ideas were presented. To date, this Client A improvement team have reduced unit-rates in excess of 40 percent—resulting in significant productivity improvements to the company as a whole, not to mention the dollars contributed to the bottom line.

We do not let either failure or success of our changes impact our analysis.

It is important that the team responsible to innovate, the team responsible to implement, the Peer Review team, management, and any relevant stakeholders stay entirely neutral throughout the evaluation and decision-making process.

Rather, everyone involved must let the data tell the story, and even if any members have championed one particular idea, they must be willing to let it go in if the data does not substantiate its ultimate acceptance. Additionally, even if one change is directly related to one successfully implemented beforehand, it is still imperative that it be considered in complete isolation from its predecessor.

Remember the story of Thomas Edison? It reportedly took him 1,000 tries before he developed a successful prototype for the light bulb. When asked how he felt about failing 1,000 times he replied, "I didn't fail 1,000 times; the light bulb was an invention with 1,000 steps." Most people, however, avoid failure. Rather than go for those big ideas or new changes, most simply settle for status quo. Those organizations that choose to constantly play it safe will be those organizations that fail to thrive and grow. Allow your employees to think about and implement those bold ideas. Challenge them to make waves, attract attention, attempt greatness, and fail. Many successful companies actively seek out those that have a track record for both success and failure, believing that those who have survived failures have had irreplaceable experience and demonstrate perseverance. To ideate and implement excellence requires delivering risky and game changing ideas, and all of this done fearlessly and without chance of repercussions.

Also remember not to let your desire for success sway your analysis of the data. This can be tempting, especially when early indicators point to success. Be as objective as possible. Let the results make your decisions, let the numbers tell the story, not your emotions.

The LEGO Case Study According to Step 8:
Implement One Change at a Time

LEGO achieved a sensational turnaround in 2013, achieving $4.5 billion in revenues and profits of $1.5 billion, and replacing Hasbro to become the largest toy company in the world after Mattel. Under the guidance of Jurgen Knudstorp, and over the course of several years, LEGO systematically and fundamentally changed the way they operated their business. A clear 10-step action plan was developed that allowed LEGO to clearly measure and analyze the financial impacts of these steps on the overall company. The first steps included cutting 30 percent of the product offerings, reducing costs, closing theme parks and re-launching DUPLO, the preschool version of the traditional LEGO brick.

The decisive manner in which these changes were executed, along with performance being tied directly to financial metrics (such as line profitability, consumer product profitability, ROS benchmarks and targets for manufacturing costs) allowed Knudstorp and his team to make sound business decisions that ultimately restored their competitive advantage and brand prominence.

We have ensured that we completed all elements of our change, and that we have done everything we can to put the change to rest.

While it may seem obvious, many times the implementation of new changes to a system are not followed through completely, and the result is an incomplete or non-replicable impact. This step is designed to ensure that you have evaluated the best solution in its entirety, implemented it completely, and measured and tracked the impacts continuously. To not do so is inefficient and counterproductive to a culture of continuous improvement.

Step 8	IMPLEMENTATION FORM

NAME OF OPTIMAL SOLUTION SELECTED: ▷

DESCRIPTION OF CHANGES MADE:

METRICS CHOSEN TO TRACK IMPACT:

PRODUCTIVITY/ PROFIT:	▷
	▷
Impact to business goals:	▷
QUALITY:	▷
	▷
Impact to business goals:	▷
SAFETY:	▷
	▷
Impact to business	▷

$ Benefit from this change:	$	Other impact not foreseen:		
		▷	$	
$ Loss from this change:	$	Other impact not foreseen:		
NET $:	$	▷	$	
		Other impact not foreseen:		
List of actionable items :		▷	$	

Action	Who	When	Complete?

Neither failure nor success of the proposed changes have impacted our analysis.

Step 9:
Sustain a Culture of
Continuous Improvement

"Whenever man comes up with a better mousetrap,
nature immediately comes up with a better mouse."

—James Carswell

Ensure that the inertia of success or failure does not stop a culture of continuous innovation and improvement.

In order for the 9 Steps to work effectively, the **culture** of the organization implementing them must reflect an ongoing and continuous curiosity. Complacency and surrender can kill this curiosity, and creating this type of culture can be extremely difficult especially if historically your people and processes are embedded.

Step 9 is designed to ensure that your people and your ways of thinking are always asking questions, always challenging yourselves, never accepting the as-is, and ensuring that whether you fail or succeed at change or innovation does not quell the desire to constantly come up with new and better solutions. It can be exceedingly difficult to affect this type of change and the following can help you jump-start the process:

Acknowledge the difficulties. Cultural change is difficult as it forces established habits, hierarchies, processes and people to think and behave in unfamiliar ways. The knowledge that these difficulties exist is the first step to overcome them.

1. People need to understand "why" a cultural change is needed.

2. There are often limited resources dedicated to affect change.

3. People do not like change and are not motivated to do it.

4. If management and their team are not aligned on the need for change, it will not happen.

Overcome the difficulties. Overcoming hurdles to organizational change requires a unified effort and message from management, as well as the identification, empowerment and support of several key change agents:

1. Find the change agents and get them committed (this can be your system improvement team leader).

2. Get people to experience the harsh realities that are forcing the change (tie them to economic reality and dollars).

3. Move resources to those areas that will result in the biggest changes.

4. Make sure you *really* know how people are feeling about the change.

5. Encourage ideas, innovation and teamwork for the "what" and "how" of change (Step 2 and Step 6).

6. The founders of the original culture must publicly and privately embrace the change.

7. Managers need to intervene on behalf of their change agents.

8. The organization needs to shine a light on the accomplishments of the change agents.

9. Advertise successful changes.

10. Retain pride in both your original culture and successful change.

Make it stick. Ensuring the sustainability of cultural change requires the ongoing measurement and assessment of your business performance, behaviors and employee attitudes (*see #1 on checklist: Gladwell's Stickiness Factor*).

1. Make sure your new culture matches with what has worked historically.

2. Focus on a few critical behavioral shifts and put a system of accountability in place to monitor.

3. Continue to honor your current culture and people.

4. Put the right formal and informal tools in place.

5. Continue to seek out the opinions of change agents and find new ones as the organization evolves.

6. Measure and assess the effective cultural change through: business performance, critical behaviors, change milestones, and employee attitudes.

So what is a culture of continuous improvement? Let's start with a brief history of continuous improvement in order to understand both its relevance and importance. Continuous improvement (CI) is generally defined by W. Edwards Deming as "improvement initiatives that increase successes and reduce failures." More specifically, CI is defined as "a culture of sustained improvement targeting the elimination of waste in all systems and processes of an organization." CI is an integral part of improving business procedures and practices and has become indispensable in the modern business world.

The earliest developed methods of CI had little in common with its present form. According to Bhuiyan and Baghel, the initial development of the programs which would eventually evolve into modern

CI can be traced back to businesses in the 1800s. These companies were largely concerned with rewarding employees who made major organization-wide improvements, and these programs were designed to provide incentives encouraging such behavior. For example, one of these companies, the National Cash Register, implemented a forerunner of a modern CI program as early as 1894, which included "reward schemes, employee development opportunities, and improving labour-management relationships" for those who tried to improve the company (Bhuiyan and Baghel). This was only the beginning of CI's rapid expansion.

These programs had further evolved significantly by the end of the nineteenth century. By the late 1800s and extending into the early 1900s, "scientific management" became the new focus of CI, as employers began to explore the possibility of using more scientific methods to better standardize company piece rates and labor standards to improve overall performance. A more specific example of this type of CI development is the "Training within Industry" service which the American government set up during WWII. It was intended to improve national productivity by implementing "job method training," which taught job supervisors about the most basic tenets of CI to be implemented in the workplace.

These CI programs were found so successful that they were implemented in the American-led economic reconstruction of Japan following the Japanese surrender at the end of WWII. As a part of this effort, Dr. W. Edwards Deming taught fledgling Japanese industries about his general principles: working tirelessly to reduce all possible excess in production and to cultivate an environment in which individual employees could feel empowered to improve the workplace. The Japanese further developed and expanded Deming's lessons about CI in part by creating the total quality management movement and eventually molding CI into a discipline of its own "associated with organized and comprehensive methodologies," using programs to positively change the larger organization. Once CI proved a success in Japan, Deming's ideas were gradually picked up by significant American companies seeking similar improvements. The general development of CI from the early 1800s on under Deming's influence has been a largely incremental and progressive effort.

CI's modern form, however, has become much more nuanced. Bhuiyan and Baghel explain that over time, a number of more specific disciplines of CI have evolved to meet various needs in the business community, including lean manufacturing, six sigma, balanced scorecard, and lean six sigma (some of which are described in further detail in Step 4). Each of these forms provides a different tool depending upon your industry and has had a distinct developmental path, making it worthwhile to understand which might be best applicable to your organization.

One branch of modern CI is lean manufacturing, defined as "a systematic approach to identifying and eliminating waste . . . by following the product at the pull of the customer in pursuit of perfection" (Bhuiyan and Baghel). Lean manufacturing ultimately seeks to eradicate excess in all steps of the manufacturing process by reforming companies' approaches to excess and waste by implementing a new mindset: "lean thinking." Lean thinking is intended to incline companies towards savings (or cost reduction). This type of CI was initially used by the Toyota Motor Company following the end of WWII, when Taiichi Ohno, a Toyota executive, developed the Toyota production system (TPS)—or what is known as the modern precursor to today's use of TPS.

The TPS, based off of Ford's efficient conveyor belt system, became a major success and is still used in companies around the world as a way to produce an ongoing production line to better allow for flexibility in the product production process. As such, lean manufacturing has had a long and established history as an effective form of CI. Many non-manufacturing industries have since incorporated much of the lean manufacturing processes into their own organizations with significant success. *Note: I have spent many years implementing these lean practices into the engineering and construction world. Neither of these industries historically used these methodologies, but have since found its application very valuable (as well as profitable).*

A second type of modern CI practice is known as six sigma, and is defined as "an organized and systematic method for strategic process improvement and new product and service development that relies on statistical methods and the scientific method to make dramatic reductions in the customer defined defect rates." Six sigma is largely concerned with reducing problems in process quality by decreasing the amount of variation which exists in a company's production methods through "statistical process control." First used and developed by Motorola Inc. in 1986, six sigma has since proved to be extremely successful and lucrative, and today has come to be regarded as a best practice for quality improvement and has been used extensively by both major companies and smaller organizations. Six sigma, like lean manufacturing, has had an extensive and successful history in modern business.

Balanced scorecard, the third recently developed branch of CI, is a "strategic planning and management system" used to "align business activities to the vision and strategy of the organization, improve internal and external communications, and monitor organization performance against strategic goals" ('Balanced Scorecard Basics'). Combining feedback loops in both process yields and company strategy, it was formally created by Robert Kaplan and David Norton in the early 1990s, and generally is used to modernize a company's overall strategy, connect general goals with the company's financial assets, and promote organization-wide understanding of a company's mission statements and vision. Balanced scorecard is currently used by approximately half of all large American firms in the US, Asia and Europe ("Balanced Scorecard Basics"). Like the other branches of CI, it has become very influential and has been proven a success in business.

The final branch of CI, lean six sigma, represents a combination or "hybrid methodology" of the lean manufacturing and six sigma approaches. Lean six sigma takes the elements of speed and continuous production from lean manufacturing and the elements of process improvement and problem-solving from six sigma, and combines them to effectively create a new type of CI which promotes speedier process improvement and an increase in quality of product or service Developed by large business groups in order to more effectively control greater shares of market space, it is a relatively new approach reflecting the ongoing spirit of innovation in CI as it continually finds new and more effective ways to improve business efficiency.

No matter which of the CI methodologies you prefer, the concept is simple: continuously find ways to improve the efficiency and productivity of your organization, and you will be able to both sustain and grow your profitability. Your organization will no longer fall victim to the trade-off between revenue growth and margin erosion. Employees can be empowered to find solutions, and managers can rest assured that there is a sound business case for change. The 9 Steps found here are yet another hybrid (and far more simplified version) of continuous improvement, coupled with sound decision-making *tied directly to the business goal of making money* that will enable your organization to achieve better performance, productivity and, ultimately, profit.

Use the following checklist to ensure that you are actively engaged both as a leader and a team-member in promoting a culture of continuous improvement. Step 9 is your feedback loop. It ensures that you continuously return to Step 1 and continue the process of seeking new and better ways to improve your business.

STEP 9 CHECKLIST

- We have implemented an ongoing process that ensures we continuously analyze our system for further improvements.
- We have reviewed our system after the changes and have identified the new bottleneck.
- Once we have identified any new bottleneck, we go back to Step 1.
- Our stakeholders are actively promoting ideas, respect, trust, and involvement.
- We are actively, as individuals and in teams, encouraging a culture of innovation where our performance is measured, reviewed, and improved.
- We understand and adhere to the previous 9 Steps in order to continuously improve our business.

We have implemented an ongoing process that ensures we continuously analyze our system for further improvements.

Once you have improved a system it is easiest to sit back and assume that it is "fixed." Instead, challenge yourself and your team to analyze your system constantly for opportunities for improvement. This can be very difficult, as once the energy and effort have been expended to make an improvement, most people find it difficult to maintain this momentum. Being creative and thoughtful requires effort and can be exhausting. It is much easier to take a break and assume you have done everything you can to fix the ultimate problem. Yet, new problems pop up every time an old one is "solved."

According to *The Goal*, this process is defined the following way:

1. Identify all of the system's bottlenecks

2. Decide how to exploit the bottlenecks

3. Subordinate everything else to the above decision.

4. Elevate the system's bottlenecks

5. If, in a previous step, a bottleneck has been broken, go back to step 1.

In other words, you should constantly and continuously be looking for your system bottlenecks in an ongoing and repetitive manner—essentially until it becomes part of your culture to do so. These 9 Steps can become part of your organizational culture in a very simple way: use the forms and the steps identified herein on a regular basis, asking both employees and managers to engage in a thoughtful exchange of ideas to improve your organization. A culture of continuous improvement no longer needs to be a formalized, expert-driven affair. It can now be utilized by every single employee at any point of operation within your company.

With the purchase of this book you have been provided with links to blank 9 Step forms. Feel free to modify them to fit your organization. Use them as a starting point to get the conversation going. Each of these forms has been tried and approved by several organizations just like yours. The process works. Now all you need to do is begin.

There is a second, and equally important, factor in your quest to create a continuous improvement culture. It is equivalent to the "stickiness factor" identified in *The Tipping Point* by Malcolm Gladwell. His research suggests there are very specific tools you can use to make your message contagious within your organization. With relatively simple changes to your structure and presentation of information, leaders can effect a large impact on how it is received.

Gladwell references several studies in both television and marketing to bolster his case, including *Sesame Street*. He suggests that the success of *Sesame Street* was neither by chance or accident, but rather through testing by the producers to test whether or not their show was holding children's attention. Gladwell concludes that in order for something to stick, it must be both practical and personal in order to become memorable. This finding hit home for me and was one of the reasons behind the development of the 9 Steps. In my experience, processes that are too complex and are messaged incorrectly tend to fail or lose steam. On the other hand, those that are "practical and personal" tend to stick.

Therefore, in order to make the implementation of 9 Steps "stick," remember to constantly monitor its progress and acceptance, hold focus groups to discuss the 9 Steps process alone, modify and improve your own 9 Steps methodology and forms, and learn from your internal people how to influence those within your employee population. A few internal champions with positive and influential voices can significantly alter both the rate of acceptance and effectiveness of the overall program.

We have reviewed our system after the changes and have identified the new bottleneck.

The 9 Steps were developed to provide you with a process and methodology that is straightforward and simple to follow—as compared to not knowing where to start. In other words, once you have reached Step 9 (for **one** system improvement) the concept is to go back to the beginning of the process and follow the order of the steps once again. The 9 Steps methodology is consistent with many well-established business practices (and in fact draws liberally from them) such as The Theory of Constraints, process and productivity improvement tools such as DMAIC and Kaizen, as well as best practices found in brainstorming, innovation, change management and continuous improvement (Lean, Six Sigma, Balanced Scorecard). The idea here is to

NOT need to be an expert in any one of those areas, but to use the consistency of thinking available within all of them. And, at the end of any system improvement, go find the next one!

Once we have identified any new bottleneck, we go back to Step 1.

The emphasis must be placed on those bottlenecks within the system that most significantly impact your **business goals** and not on areas that have little to no impact on these two or three critical factors. This emphasis on decisions that impact the financial (and other key) business goals of the organization must continuously be reinforced. This must be emphasized over and over throughout the 9 Steps process, as it is tempting to bypass any one of the steps. To do so, however, eliminates the checks and balances inherent in the process.

This is a message that must be reinforced by management and change leaders. In fact, managers, leaders and system improvement teams must thoroughly and completely understand each of the 9 Steps in order to implement them effectively. Reading this book in its entirety is very important to those leading the teams that will utilize the 9 Steps. The forms and checklists are designed to make it simple and easy to use for those that may not want to understand the research and development behind it. In my experience, a combined approach is most effective.

In my many years of consulting and research developing these 9 Steps, I have found that almost everyone at any level of any organization is both interested and wants to engage in the process. One of my favorite memories is of a young woman sending me an email asking for some blank forms because she had ideas on how to "fix" her department. She was 22 and had worked there for six months. I thought that was great.

STEP 9—IN THE REAL WORLD

For Client A, the key to sustaining a culture of continuous improvement is an ongoing adherence to the 9 Steps. Clear and consistent documentation, ongoing, frequent, and consistent communication, a structured Peer Review process, and the continuous introduction of new and innovative ideas is the only way to sustain growth and profitability of the business.

By making sound and innovative business decisions together, the management and employees of Client A are able to focus on those few critical behavioral shifts and hold each other accountable to business performance, employee attitudes and those change milestones that will secure a vibrant and successful future.

Client A continues to implement 9 Steps today.

Our stakeholders are actively promoting ideas, respect, trust, and involvement.

Key to the entire cultural effort is the attitude and messages being observed and received from stakeholders within the organization. Senior management must buy-in, embrace and promote the culture, team leaders must actively set aside time to review and improve systems, and employees must feel secure in the knowledge that their ideas and creativity are to be heard and rewarded. We discussed this in detail in Step 8 (using the DICE model) about how important this buy-in to new projects and ideas is to the organization. Just as importantly, these very same individuals need to embrace the entire culture of continuous improvement, the big ideas, innovation, and financially-driven, sound business decisions inherent in the 9 Steps process.

Once your organization has begun the 9 Steps process, make sure senior management has a discussion around these concepts of respect, trust and involvement. Seriously analyze whether or not your current culture embraces this way of operating, and if not, keep in mind that you will need to actively work on these "soft" elements as much as (if not more) than the 9 Steps themselves. Simply put: your employees will not bring their ideas for improvement to you if they do not intrinsically feel trusted, respected and involved. Only then will a cultural shift be possible and ultimately sustainable.

In my experience both metrics and accountability contribute substantially to a culture of respect, trust and involvement. When employees do not have clear expectations or goals, it is difficult for them to engage meaningfully. Additionally, when managers and peers hold each other accountable to commitments and performance, it builds rather than erodes a continuous improvement culture (see next step).

We are actively, as individuals and in teams, encouraging a culture of innovation where our performance is measured, reviewed and improved.

It is also important that managers and leaders hold their teams accountable not only to an attitude of continuous improvement, but a process whereby performance is measured and reviewed. Performance metrics should be tied to the system and its impact on *business goals* rather than individual performance metrics that may or may not have any direct influence on the *actual* business objectives of the organization. Metrics and accountability are key to this process. Without them, it will not work. Metrics are designed to be objective, not personal, and remove any bias or emotion from the process. Measurement through metrics and reviewing and decision-making based on empirical data is a fair and efficient way to run your organization, and the majority of employees prefer this way of operation.

Many years ago I worked within an organization where the CEO based every one of his decisions upon who brought the idea to him and whether or not you were in "favor" or "not in favor" at the time with him. Not one of the employees knew at any given time if their suggestions were good or bad, if they were to be implemented or not, and ultimately, where they stood. They did not feel respected, trusted, or involved. Instead, the culture was one of isolationism, fear and distrust. It was a miserable place to work, most of the employees left within a short time after being hired, and the company folded despite an intriguing and market worthy product.

As such, teams and managers should work together to establish these performance metrics and reward and recognize improvements to that team's or individual's "system" where appropriate. Without this tie-in, it is virtually impossible to sustain a culture of continuous improvement, as employees will ultimately feel disconnected and/or disenchanted. System improvement team leaders must watch for this vigilantly and act accordingly when either the 9 Steps are being dismissed or skipped over, or when idea flow stops.

We understand and adhere to the previous 9 Steps in order to continuously improve our business.

The potential benefits to be gained from a successful transition to a continuous-improvement culture are many, particularly including the potential generation of hundreds of millions of dollars in new opportunities. A truly successful implementation of 9 Steps throughout the culture of any organization will prevent a company from becoming stagnant, continually elevating the organization's internal functions and processes to capture new technologies and perform at the peak of its industry. These 9 Steps will allow a company to continually reinvent itself, challenge employees to strive for better performance, and maintain product and service offerings at the lowest cost with highest quality and best service for customers.

With a simple shift in organizational culture and process, a company can realize highly advantageous outcomes.

However, keep in mind that more than sixty percent of efforts to transition to a CI organizational structure ultimately fail. That is because the transition from an organizational structure not utilizing CI practices to one which uses CI as an integral part of company improvement is extremely challenging. It is not enough to artificially add yet another program to your company and stop there – the changes that must be made in order to ensure ongoing success are extremely deep and must substantially alter the very innermost workings of an organization. These changes can be hindered by ongoing evolutions in the modern workplace such as the growing need for specifically skilled workers to perform ad hoc work, rapidly evolving manufacturing, software and internal processes, an increasingly variable workforce, and the potential power of "big data."

That said, in order for the 9 Steps to be effective, the proper training and understanding of its language and intent must be provided throughout the organization, otherwise it will be viewed as "just another new plan." Once your organization has embarked upon these 9 Steps, understanding the inherent challenge of implementing a new way of thinking and operating must be discussed, understood, planned for and communicated.

As mentioned at the beginning of Step 9, creating a culture of continuous improvement is different than implementing a program around continuous improvement. The distinction is important, for even if the proper capital is expended, a great software program is installed, experts are brought in and the right language is bandied about, an organization will not embrace and sustain this way of thinking without the people buying-in to this new way of running the business.

In this chapter we have identified several methodologies for an extensive CI program (lean, six sigma, balanced scorecard, lean six sigma) all of which are valuable and effective processes. However, some of these can be complex and difficult to implement depending upon the level of expertise within your organization. 9 Steps can be used in conjunction with any of these formal programs, or as a stand-alone process.

The 9 Steps were designed to remove the need to be an expert or to bring in outside help. It was designed to be a process that is simple to implement using the checklists and forms provided for both employees and managers. It does not require extensive training other than a basic understanding of the driving forces behind each of the steps and adherence to the checklists and chronology. It does not require outside experts to come in and first learn your operation and culture, then spend an inordinate amount of time developing and training new processes. It utilizes the already existent expertise within your company and relies on your very own people to implement the changes. It creates a culture of ownership, vested interest, financial sophistication, and sound decisions. However, like any process it must be accepted and embraced by the people who use it.

This acceptance cannot mean that this approach is solely a top-down driven business initiative; it must be a wholesale approach to all internal processes and procedures within the organization, with everyone's involvement—and most especially by those who actually perform the work within the system. This cultural shift is critical to your success.

The LEGO Case Study According to Step 9:
Sustain a Culture of Continuous Improvement

LEGO is now widely considered to be the "Apple of Toys." LEGO has built a culture of continuous improvement (and innovation around sound business decisions) primarily by way of being a profit-driven, design-generating organization full of creative thinkers, Future Lab, crowdsourcing for future ideas, and an open door policy for staff, retailers, and other visitors both seeking inspiration and offering new ideas.

Despite a deep process-based thinker at the helm (Knudstorp), the team responsible for LEGO has built an organization where "everything is awesome!"

Step 9	CONTINUOUS IMPROVEMENT FORM

Documentation of our findings can be found here: (FDR's, research, time studies, ROI's, etc.)	▶
Results summary:	▶
We will communicate our findings/results to the company in the following way:	▶
We think the next bottleneck/inefficiency within our system is:	▶
Proposed Step 1 start date:	▶

Resources

Step 1: Identify the System Which Needs Improvement

Ashcroft, J. (2014, April 14). *The Lego Case Study, The Great Turnaround 2003-2013*. From http://de.slideshare.net/jkaonline/the-lego-case-study-the-great-turn-around-2003-2013

Collins, J. C. (2001). *Good to Great*. New York, NY: HarperCollins Publishers, Inc.

Deming, W. E. (2015, August 26). *Are You Sustaining a Culture of Continuous Improvement?*. From http://www.leading2lean.com/are-you-sustaining-a-culture-of-continuous-improvement/

Drucker, P. F., Collins, J. C., Kotler, P., Kouzes, J., Rodin, J., Rangan, K. V., & Hesselbein, F. (2008). *The Five Most Important Questions You Will Ever Ask About Your Organization*. San Francisco, CA: Jossey-Bass, a Wiley Imprint.

Gladwell, M. T. (2000). *The Tipping Point: How Little Things Make a Big Difference*. New York, NY: Little, Brown and Company.

Harvard Business Review Staff. (2013, November). *You Can't Be a Wimp-Make the Tough Calls*. From https://hbr.org/2013/11/you-cant-be-a-wimp-make-the-tough-calls

Ringer, J. (2015, January 8). *How Lego Became the Apple of Toys*. From http://www.fastcompany.com/3040223/when-it-clicks-it-clicks

Spencer Johnson, S., (1998). *Who Moved My Cheese*. New York, NY: G.P. Putnam's Sons.

Taleb, N. N. (2010). *The Black Swan*. New York, NY: Random House Trade Paperbacks.

Managing a Business—Making Decisions. (n.d.) From https://www.sba.gov/managing-business/leading-your-business/making-decisions.

Step 2: Put the Right Team Together

Buckingham, M., & Clifton, D. O. (2001). Now, Discover Your Strengths. New York, NY: The Free Press.

Cialdini, R. B. (2001, October). *Harnessing the Science of Persuasion*. From https://hbr.org/2001/10/harnessing-the-science-of- persuasion

Dorsey, J. R. (2010). *Y-Size Your Business: How Gen Y Employees Can Save You Money and Grow Your Business*. Hoboken, New Jersey: John Wiley & Sons, Inc.

Gladwell, M.T. (2005). *Blink: The Power of Thinking Without Thinking*. New York, NY: Little, Brown and Company.

Kim, W. C., & Mauborgne, R. (2005). *Blue Ocean Strategy: How to Create Uncontested Market Space and Make the Competition Irrelevant.* Boston, Massachusetts: Harvard Business School Publishing Corporation.

Pentland, A. (2013, November) *Beyond the Echo Chamber.* From https://hbr.org/2013/11/beyond-the-echo-chamber

Rath, T., & Conchie, B. (2008). *Strengths Based Leadership: Great Leaders, Teams, and Why People Follow.* New York, NY: Gallup Press.

Ringer, J. (2015, January 8). How Lego Became the Apple of Toys. From http://www.fastcompany.com/3040223/when-it-clicks-it-clicks

Straw, J. & Cerier, A. B. (2002). *The 4-Dimensional Manager.* San Francisco, California: Berrett-Koehler Publishers, Inc.

Stuart, C. (1996). *How to be an Effective Speaker: The Essential Guide to Making the Most of Your Communication Skills.* Chicago, Illinois: NTC Publishing Group.

Step 3: Identify the Goal

Ashcroft, J. (2014, April 14). *The Lego Case Study, The Great Turnaround 2003-2013.* From http://de.slideshare.net/jkaonline/the-lego-case-study-the-great-turnaround-2003-2013

Campbell, A. (1999, March). *Tailored but not Benchmarked: A Fresh Look at Corporate Planning.* From https://hbr.org/1999/03/tailored-not-benchmarked-a-fresh-look- at-corporate-planning

Drucker, P. F., Collins, J. C., Kotler, P., Kouzes, J., Rodin, J., Rangan, K. V., & Hesselbein, F. (2008). *The Five Most Important Questions You Will Ever Ask About Your Organization.* San Francisco, CA: Jossey-Bass, a Wiley Imprint.

Hartman, N., (2014, February 5). *Seven Steps to Running the Most Effective Meeting Possible.* From http://www.forbes.com/sites/forbesleadershipforum/2014/02/05/seven-steps-to-running-the-most -effective-meeting- possible/#735df9661054

Lotich, P. (2016, May 11). *8 Steps for Creating a Customer Service System.* From http://thethrivingsmallbusiness.com/customer-service-as-a-system/

Mankins, M., Brahm, C., & Caimi, G. (2016, June 20). *Your Scarcest Resource.* From https://hbr.org/2014/05/your-scarcest- resource

Ringer, J. (2015, January 8). How Lego Became the Apple of Toys. From http://www.fastcompany.com/3040223/when-it-clicks-it-clicks

Robins, C. (May 30) *10 Rules for Successful Mergers and Acquisitions.* From http://linqpartners.com/blog/2016/05/30/10-rules-for-successful -mergers-and-acquisitions/

Rue, L. W., & Lloyd Byars, L. L. (2003). *Management Skills and Application, 10th Edition.* New York, NY: McGraw-Hill Irwin.

(2015). *Lego was off track and management didn't really understand how far it was off.* From https://www.coursehero.com/file/p30vn3t/Lego-was-off-track-and -management-didnt-really-understand-how-far-it-was-off/

(n.d.). *Challenges of Supervising a Diverse Workforce.*
From http://www.markedbyteachers.com/university-degree/business-and
-administrative-studies/challenges-of-supervising-a-diverse-workforce.html

(n.d.). *High-performance teams.* From https://en.wikipedia.org/wiki/High
-performance_teams

Step 4: Observe the System

Bradbury,J. (2016, July 1). *What is Kaizen?.* From https://www.graphicproducts.com/
articles/what-is-kaizen/

Courtney, H., Lovallo, D., &Clarke, C. (2013, November). *Deciding How to Decide.*
From https://hbr.org/2013/11/deciding-how-to-decide

Fox, T. (2016, March 15). *Kaizen for Compliance.* From https://www.linkedin.com/
pulse/kaizen-compliance-thomas-fox

Gladwell, M. T. (2008). *Outliers: The Story of Success.* New York, NY: Little, Brown
and Company.

Kaplan, R.S., & Norton, D.P. (2005, July). *The Balanced Scorecard: Measures That
Drive Performance.* From https://hbr.org/2005/07/the-balanced-scorecard
-measures-that-drive-performance

Magno, C. (2014, June 30). *The Use of Assessment Information: Root Cause Analysis.*
From http://www.slideshare.net/crlmgn/root-cause-analysis-36472288

Pai, V., (2015, July 5).Six Sigma and Information Security.
From https://www.linkedin.com/pulse/six-sigma-information-security
-vishant-pai Robert W. Hall, R. W. (1987). *Attaining Manufacturing
Excellence: Just In Time, Total Quality, Total People Involvement.* Homewood,
Illinois: Business One Irwin.

Reid, R. D., & Sanders, N. R. (2002). *Operations Management.* New York, NY:
John Wiley & Sons, Inc.

Ringer, J. (2015, January 8). How Lego Became the Apple of Toys.
From http://www.fastcompany.com/3040223/when-it-clicks-it-clicks

Williams, M., (2016, February 21). *Lean Six Sigma.* From https://prezi.com/qejn4
_enup3u/lean-six-sigma-an-introduction/

(2015, February 10). *Anatomy of a CI Project: Adopting the DMAIC Model.* From
https://prezi.com/jsquxdc4pi_c/anatomy-of-a-ci-project/

(2015, March 23). *Improving Nurse Scheduling in Operating Rooms using Lean
Principles – How It Can Optimize Costs.* From http://www.slideshare.net/
WilliamReau/lean-scheduling-in-operating-rooms-46173029

(2016, May 30). *The Bank Holiday basics of Lean and Six Sigma.*
From http://investorsinexcellence.com/news/bank-holiday-basics-lean
-six-sigma/

(n.d.).*DMAIC.* From https://en.wikipedia.org/wiki/DMAIC

(n.d.). *The DMAIC Process.* From http://www.spiexperts.com/Sigma.html

(n.d.). *DMAIC.* From https://www.edrawsoft.com/templates/pdf/dmaic-diagram.pdf

(n.d.). *DMAIC Steps.* From https://dmaic-dmaic.com/dmaic-steps/

(n.d.).*Fundamentals of Quality.* From http://courses.aiu.edu/Fundamentals%20 of%20Quality.html

(n.d.). *Introduction to DMAIC: The DMAIC Improvement Process.* From https://adaptivebms.com/Introduction_to_DMAIC/

(n.d.). *Lean Management.* From http://www.kanbanchi.com/lean-management

(n.d.). *Lean Six Sigma Green Belt Certification Program.* From https://ctme.caltech.edu/project-management/lean-six-sigma -green-belt-certificate-caltech

(n.d.). *Organisational Planning Tools.* From http://ibnotesbyellie.weebly.com/ organisational-planning-tools.html

(n.d.). *Root Cause Analysis.* From https://en.wikipedia.org/wiki/Root_cause _analysis

(n.d.). *Root Cause Analysis.* From http://www.imiconsultant.com/main-service/ root-cause-analysis/

(n.d.).*Six Sigma and Organizational Goal.* From http://www.vskills.in/certification/ tutorial/quality/six-sigma-green-belt/six-sigma-and-organizational-goal/

(n.d.). *The DMAIC Improvement Process.* From https://www.scribd.com/ doc/306030809/The-DMAIC-Improvement-Process

(n.d.). *The Five Steps of DMAIC.* From http://paceimpact.com/about-us/what-is -lean/five-steps-dmaic/

(n.d.). *How to Use Lean Principles: To Improve Scheduling in Health Systems and Reduce Costs While Increasing Value.* From http://hallmarkhealthcareit.com/ downloads/lean-scheduling-how-to-use-lean-principles.pdf

(n.d.). *QI Tool—Fishbone Diagram.* From http://www.etsu.edu/com/familymed/ researchdivision/improvement/Fishbone_Diagram.aspx

(n.d.). *What is Fishbone Diagram.* From http://whatis.techtarget.com/definition/ fishbone-diagram

Step 5: Identify Bottlenecks within the System

Cox, J., Houle, D., & Cole, H., (2014). *Hanging Fire: Achieving Predictable Results in an Uncertain World.* CreateSpace Independent Publishing Platform.

Goldratt, E. M., & Cox, J., (1992). *The Goal: A Process of Ongoing Improvement. Second Edition.* New York, NY: North River Press.

Hall, R. W., (1987). *Attaining Manufacturing Excellence: Just In Time, Total Quality, Total People Involvement.* Homewood, Illinois: Business One Irwin.

Pratt, A. R., (2015, November 18). *Performance Improvement—A Five-Step Process Begins with the Bottleneck.* From http://www.fgmk.com/performance-improvement-a-five-step

Ringer, J. (2015, January 8). How Lego Became the Apple of Toys. From http://www.fastcompany.com/3040223/when-it-clicks-it-clicks

Stevenson, S., (n.d.).*When Did We Manage to Buy the NCX-10?*. From http://www.slate.com/articles/business/operations/2012/06/the _goal_eli_goldratt_s_gripping_thriller_about_operations_theory_. html-process-begins-with-the-bottleneck/

Step 6: Brainstorm

Anchor, S., (2010). *The Happiness Advantage*. New York, NY: Crown Business, A Division of Random House.

Callahan, S., (2006, September 16). *Eight Rules to Brilliant Brainstorming*. From http://www.anecdote.com/2006/09/eight-rules-brilliant-brainstorming/

Charan, R., (2008). *Leaders at All Levels*. San Francisco, California: Jossey-Bass, a Wiley Imprint.

Cialdini, R. B., (2001, October). *Harnessing the Science of Persuasion*. From https://hbr.org/2001/10/harnessing-the-science-of- persuasion.

Dorsey, J. R., (2010). *Y-Size Your Business: How Gen Y Employees Can Save You Money and Grow Your Business*. Hoboken, New Jersey: John Wiley & Sons, Inc.

Deutch, M., (2013, July 16).*Tips and Tricks for Team Brainstorming*. From http://blog.mindjet.com/2013/07/team-brainstorming-tips/

Kabani, S., (2013, October 15). *5 Ways to be More Innovative in the Digital Age*. From http://www.forbes.com/sites/groupthink/2013/10/15/5-ways-to-be -more-innovative-in-the-digital-age/#18d0498b689a

Kim, W. C., & Mauborgne, R. (2005). *Blue Ocean Strategy: How to Create Uncontested Market Space and Make the Competition Irrelevant*. Boston, Massachusetts: Harvard Business School Publishing Corporation.

Pasick, R., & O'Gorman, K., (2009). *Balanced Leadership in Unbalanced Times*. Canton, Michigan: David Crumm Media, LLC.

Rackham, N., Friedman, L. M., & Ruff, R., (1996). *Getting Partnering Right*. New York, NY: McGraw-Hill Company.

Ringer, J. (2015, January 8). How Lego Became the Apple of Toys. From http://www.fastcompany.com/3040223/when-it-clicks- it-clicks

Straw, J. & Cerier, A. B. (2002). *The 4-Dimensional Manager*. San Francisco, California: Berrett-Koehler Publishers, Inc.

Sutton, R.I., (2006, July 25). *Eight Tips for Better Brainstorming*. From http://www.bloomberg.com/news/articles/2006-07-25/eight-tips -for-better-brainstorming

(2006, September 24). *Eight Rules to Brilliant Brainstorming*. From http://www.bloomberg.com/news/articles/2006-09-24/eight -rules-to-brilliant-brainstorming

(2011, February 4). *Feb 2 Eight Tips for Better Brainstorming.*
From http://suwinter2011.blogspot.com/

(n.d.). *High-performance teams.*
From https://en.wikipedia.org/wiki/High-performance_teams

(n.d.).*Running head: met ad 715 assignment 1 ensure that they are focusing on the goal.*
From https://www.coursehero.com/file/p5qov38/Running-Head-MET
-AD-715-Assignment-1-ensure-that-they-are-focusing-on-the-goal/

Step 7: Select Optimal Solutions for Improvement

Aravossis, K. G., (2003, January). *Program Evaluation Methodologies: A Comparative Assessment.* From https://www.researchgate.net/publication/228434062_
Program_Evaluation_Methodologies_A_Comparative_Assessment

Collins, J. C. (2001). *Good to Great.* New York, NY: HarperCollins Publishers, Inc.

Denning, S., (2011, July 23). *How Do You Change an Organizational Culture?,*
From https://www.yahoo.com/news/change-organizational-
culture-220941086.html

Grossman, J., (2012, December 24). *The Difference Between a Good and Bad Place to Work.* From http://jaygrossman.com/post/2012/12/24/The-Difference
-between-a-Good-and-Bad-Place-to-Work.aspx

Hall, R.W., (1987). *Attaining Manufacturing Excellence: Just In Time, Total Quality, Total People Involvement.* Homewood, Illinois: Business One Irwin.

Hess, E. D., & Liedtka, J. M., (2012). , *The Physics of Business Growth: Mindsets, System, and Processes.* Stanford, California: Stanford University Press.

Ringer, J. (2015, January 8). How Lego Became the Apple of Toys.
From http://www.fastcompany.com/3040223/when-it-clicks-it-clicks

Schoemaker, P. J. H., Krupp,S., & Howland, S., (2013, January). *Strategic Leadership: The Essential Skills.*
From https://hbr.org/2013/01/strategic-leadership-the-esssential-skills

Treacy, M., & Wiersema, F., (1995). *The Discipline of Market Leaders.* Boston, MA: Addison-Wesley.

Step 8: Implement One Change at a Time

Bossidy, L. A., & Charan,R.,(2002). *Execution: The Discipline of Getting Things Done.* New York, NY: Crown Business.

Gladwell, M. T., (2000). *The Tipping Point: How Little Things Make a Big Difference.* New York, NY: Little, Brown and Company.

Morris, S., & Morris,J., (2003). *Leadership Simple: Leading People to Lead Themselves.* Santa Barbara, California: Imporex International.

Ringer, J. (2015, January 8). How Lego Became the Apple of Toys.
From http://www.fastcompany.com/3040223/when-it-clicks- it- clicks

Treacy, M., & Wiersema, F., (1995). *The Discipline of Market Leaders*. New York, NY: Perseus Publishing.

Step 9: Sustain a Culture of Continuous Improvement

Achor, S., (2013). *Before Happiness*. New York, NY: Crown Business, a Division of Random House.

Bhuiyan, N., & Baghel, A.,(n.d.). *An Overview of Continuous Improvement: From the past to the Present.* From http://www.iem.unifei.edu.br/turrioni/PosGraduacao/PQM07/Continuous_improvement_aula_4_e_5/0010430509%20melhoria%20continua.pdf

Brafman, O., & Beckstrom, R., (2006). *The Starfish and the Spider: The Unstoppable Power of Leaderless Organizations*. London, England: Penguin Books Ltd.

Ciampa, D., & Watkins, M. D., (1999). *Right From the Start: Taking Charge in a New Leadership Role*. Boston, Massachusetts: Harvard Business School Press. Morris, S., &

Collins, J.C., (2009). *How the Mighty Fall and Why Some Companies Never Give In*. New York, NY: HarperCollins Publishers, Inc.

Dungy, A. K., & Whitaker, N., (2007). *Quiet Strength: The Principles, Practices, and Priorities of a Winning Life*. Carol Stream, Illinois: Tyndale House Publishers.

Hindery, L., Jr.,(2005). *It Takes a CEO: It's Time to Lead With Integrity*. New York, NY: Free Press.

Holusha, J. (1993, December 21) *W. Edwards Deming, Expert on Business Management, Dies at 9.* From http://www.nytimes.com/1993/12/21/obituaries/w-edwards-deming-expert-on-business-management-dies-at-93.html?pagewanted=all

Katzenbach, J. R., Steffen, I., & Kronley, C.,(2012, July). *Cultural Change That Sticks.* From https://hbr.org/2012/07/cultural-change- that-sticks

Kotter, J. P., (2012, September 27). *The Key to Changing Organizational Culture.* From http://www.forbes.com/sites/johnkotter/2012/09/27/the-key-to-changing- organizational-culture/#1db676507238

McInnis, D., (n.d.). W. Edwards Deming of Powell, Wyo.: The Man Who Helped Shape the World. From http://www.wyohistory.org/encyclopedia/w-edwards-deming

Morris,J., (2003). *Leadership Simple: Leading People to Lead Themselves*. Santa Barbara, California: Imporex International.

Murray, A. (n.d.). *How to Change Your Organization's Culture.* From http://guides.wsj.com/management/innovation/how-to-change-your-organizations-culture/

Oakley, S. J.,(n.d.). *Vuilding a culture of continuous improvement in an age of disruption.* From http://www2.deloitte.com/content/dam/Deloitte/us/Documents/process-and-operations/us-cons-continuous-improvement-052714.pdf

Pasick, R., & O'Gorman, K., (2009). *Balanced Leadership in Unbalanced Times.* Canton, Michigan: David Crumm Media, LLC.

Ringer, J. (2015, January 8). How Lego Became the Apple of Toys. From http://www.fastcompany.com/3040223/when-it-clicks-it-clicks

Sirkin, H. L., Keenan, P., & Jackson,A. E.(2005, October). *The Hard Side of Change Management.* From https://hbr.org/2005/10/the-hard-side-of -change-management

(n.d.).Balanced Scorecard. From http://balancedscorecardtanzania.com/

(n.d.). *Balanced Scorecard Basics.* From http://balancedscorecard.org/Resources/ About-the-Balanced-Scorecard

(n.d.). *Building a Culture of Continuous Improvement in an Age of Disruption.* From. http://www2.deloitte.com/content/dam/Deloitte/us/Documents/ process-and-operations/us-cons-continuous-improvement-052714.pdf

(n.d.).*Building Customer Satisfaction.* From http://www.appliedmaterials.com/en-sg/node/3342910

(n.d.). *History of Six Sigma.* From http://www.greycampus.com/opencampus/ lean-six-sigma-green-belt/history-of-six-sigma

(n.d.). *What Is Lean Six Sigma?,.* From http://www.leansixsigmainstitute.org/ #!what-is-lss/c18pr

Index

Accounting, 58–59
Action items
    follow-up, 39–40
    rules, 39–40
Ad hoc work, performing, 189
Agendas
    rules, 39
    usage, 39–40
Aha moment, 96–97
Alternatives, 31, 37–38
Analysis tool, usage, 74–87
Analytical bias, 88–89
Analytical tools, usage (reason), 150
Analyze, 83–84. *See also* Define,
    measure, analyze, improve,
    control
Apple, comeback, 35
Applied Immigration (Osborn), 113
Assembly-based RCA, 78
Audience
    assumptions, 89
    feedback, 90
Audit, absence, 103
Aurelius, Marcus, 65
Automation, 85

Balanced Scorecard, 184, 189–190
    Basics, 180
Behavioral shifts, focus, 177
Benchmarking, examples
    (consideration), 117, 127–128
Best practices, examples
    (consideration), 127–128
"Beyond the Echo Chamber"
    (Pentland), 24
Bias
    checklist, 119, 123
    team avoidance, 117, 119–120
    impact, 127

Big data, power, 189
Bleed effects, 14
Blink (Gladwell), 28
Blue Ocean Strategy (Kim/
    Mauborgne), 24, 128
Bottlenecks, 76, 97
    breakage, 183
    capacity, increase, 125, 130
    checklist, 99
    definition, 10, 70
        understanding, 97–99
    elevation, 183
    example, 95
    existence, identification, 102
    exploitation, 183
    form, identification, 109–110
    identification, 5, 12, 93, 99,
        182–185
        experience, 100–101
        LEGO case study, 107–108
    impact, identification, 103–104
    root causes, impact, 102–103
    term, understanding, 98
    verification, mathematical
        evaluation (usage), 106
Boundaries
    definition, 10
    identification, 14–15
    upstream/downstream
        boundaries, 140
Brainstorming, 5, 111
    checklist, 117
    efforts, documentation, 117,
        129–130
    example, 126
    face-to-face brainstorms,
        guidelines (Sutton), 112–114

fear, impact, 113
filibusters, 118
form, 132
ideas, business goals alignment,
    130
individual brainstorming, usage,
    113
ineffectiveness, 14
LEGO case study, 131
meeting, example, 38–39
outcome, documentation,
    129–130
outputs, prioritization, 137–145
process, ideas list (reduction),
    121
rules, 114
sessions, 168–169
    competitiveness, 113–114
    value, 113
    skill/experience, requirement,
        113
    system improvement team
        development, 118
    usage, 77, 112
Breakthrough innovation strategy,
    116
Business
    continuous improvement,
        188–190
    elements, 49–50
    performance, 177
    positive impact, reduction, 105
Business goals, 49
    brainstorming ideas, alignment,
        130
    changes
        alignment, 125
        impact, 138
    changes, impact, 60
    definition, 9–10
    impact, 137–145, 185
    improvement, system
        improvement (impact),
        13–14

metrics, relationship, 53, 56–60
monetization, 137
owners, feedback, 11
    request, 15
problems, 55–56
relationship, 53
understanding, 53, 62
    Capital investment, usage
        (example), 146
Carswell, James, 175
Change, 94
    advertisement, 176
    bleed effects, 14
    consequences, documentation,
        169
    double-checking, 149–150
    elements, completion, 173
    embracing, 176
    failure/success, impact (absence),
        164, 171
    impact
        analysis, 146–148
        documentation, 168–169
    milestones, 177
    organizational level,
        management, 158–159
    recommendations, Peer Review
        group buy-in, 145–146
    system review, 184–185
    team implementation, 62
Change agent, 33–34
    accomplishments, 176
    opinions, usage, 177
Change implementation, 5, 157, 165
    checklist, 164
    decision-maker approval, 164–
        165
    example, 170
    form, 174
    LEGO case study, 172
    management buy-in, 138, 146
    team accountability, 43
Closed-loop system, 41

Commitment, 161–162
  types, 162
Communication/cooperation,
  improvement, 86
Communication plan, 158
Community relations, 50–51
Company
  personal investment, provision,
    87
  productivity, face-to-face
    interactions (impact), 24
Competition, impact, 33
Constraints
  Theory of Constraints, 93–95,
    184
    language, example, 138–139
    usage, 103–104
  types, 102
  understanding, 98
Continuous improvement (CI), 85
  achievement, 85
  change, 178–179
  checklist, 182
  culture
    creation, 183–184
    sustaining, 5, 175
  definition, 10
  difficulties, acknowledgment,
    176–177
  effort, 55
  emotional components, 45
  example, 186
  form, 192
  hybrid methodology, 181
  LEGO case study, 191
  process, definition, 183
  RCA tool, 80
  sustainability, 177–181
Control, 84–85. *See also* Define,
  measure, analyze, improve,
  control
  chart, usefulness, 84–85
Cost-benefit
  analysis, 133, 149

  purpose, 136
  checklist, 137–140
  exercise, usage, 167
  quantification, 140
  ratio, assessment, 134
  system changes, measurement/
    tracking (relationship),
    167–168
Costs, reduction, 86
Crazy thinking, 118
Creative ideas, allowance, 128–129
Creative thought, negativity
  (reduction/cessation), 117, 129
Crew, information/ideas, 40–41
Critical behaviors, impact, 177
Critical to Quality (CTQ), 82
CRM system, implementation, 15
Cultural change, 147–148
  difficulties
    acknowledgment, 175–176
    overcoming, 176–177
  measurement/assessment, 177
  reason, understanding, 176
  sustainability, ensuring, 177–181
Culture
  embrace/promotion, 186–187
  honoring, 177
  pride, 177
  shocks, types, 147
  soft issue, focus, 159
Customers
  satisfaction, 50–51, 57
    improvement, 86
  team understanding, 31, 36–37
  types, 36
  voice of the customer (VOC), 82
Data
  origin, challenge, 124
DCMA, 75
Decision-makers
  approval, 164–165
  communication, 146
  focus, 14
  impact, 90

Define, 82–83
Define, measure, analyze, improve,
    control (DMAIC), 76, 150,
    184
    improvement steps, 82f
    process, data, 83
    target process, 82
Deming, W. Edwards, 177
Denning, Steve, 148
Design Services Team (SAP), 113
DICE. *See* Duration Integrity
    Commitment Employees
Disruptive innovation strategy, 117
Dissent, encouragement, 44
Distortion, detection, 127
Documentation, importance, 43, 88
Downstream boundaries, 140
Drum Buffer Rope, 104
Due diligence, completion, 17
DUPLO, relaunch, 172
Dupuit, Jules, 136
Duration, 160–161
Duration Integrity Commitment
    Employees (DICE)
    method/program, 159–163
    metrics, 165–166
    model, 186

Echo chamber
    avoidance, 31, 41
    closed system, 41
Edison, Thomas, 171
Efficiency
    decrease, 12
    improvement, 37
    increase, 167–168
Employee
    attitudes, impact, 177
    base, momentum, 45
    development opportunities, 178
    rewards, 86
    satisfaction, 87
    workload, increase, 162
    work shifts, example, 116
Engineering, definition (usage), 151
Engoron, Ed, 111

Equipment
    availability, interdependency
        type, 106
    constraints, 102
Eureka! moment, 169
Events sequence (establishment),
    RCA (usage), 81
Executive commitment, 162
Expert Loop, 24–26
    avoidance, 34
    decisions/reversion, 30
    elimination, 31
External customers, 36–37
Extroverts, domination, 38

Fabrication costs, reduction, 55
Face-to-face brainstorms, guidelines
    (Sutton), 112–114
Face-to-face interactions,
    involvement, 24
Failure
    failure-based RCA, 78, 80
    impact, 32, 44–45
    track record, 171
Fear, elimination, 74
Federal Navigation Act (1936), 136
Feedback, usage, 11, 15, 90
Field Operations Report, 69
Filtering system, 65
Final assembly building, move
    (example/solution), 143–145
Fishbone application, 76
Fishbone diagram, 75–78, 88, 106
    detail, example, 79f
    drawing, 77
    example, 78f
    usage, 103, 150
5S, 85
Floor space, reduction, 142
Food innovations, 111–112
4 Ps. *See* Place, Procedure, People,
    Policies
4 Ss. *See* Surroundings, Suppliers,
    Systems, Skills
Freud, Sigmund, 113
Future Lab (LEGO), 131

Gain, 104
Gates, Bill, 128–129
Gen Y group, ideas, 27–28
Gladwell, Malcolm, 28, 183–184
Goals. *See* Business goals
    checklist, 53
    definition, 10
    form, 64
    identification, 4, 49
      case study, 63
      example, 61
      LEGO case study, 63
    measurement, metrics (usage),
      53, 56–60
    preliminary goal, definition,
      18–19
    relationships, 53, 55–56
    setting, 62
    statement, 83
    understanding, 62
Goal, The (Goldratt), 93–96, 98, 183
    bottleneck, relationship, 97
Goldratt, Eliyahu M., 93–96, 98
Ground rules, 39–40
    rules, 39
Group sessions, individual
    brainstorming (usage), 113
Groupthink, 115
    checklist, 123
    problems, 116
    team avoidance, 117, 123
      impact, 127
Growth, 50–51
Gut check, performing, 145
Gut-check, performing, 130
Gut instinct, 28

Hard factors, 159
*Hard Facts, Dangerous Half-Truths
    and Total Nonsense* (Sutton),
    112
"Hard Side of Change Management,
    The" (Sirkin/Keenan/
    Jackson), 157
Hargadon, Andrew, 112
Herbie, 93–98

Hill, Napoleon, 49
Histograms, usage, 84
How Breakthroughs Happen
    (Hargadon), 112
Human resources, 57–58
Hybrid methodology, 181

Ideas, 31, 37–38
    brainstorming, example, 167–168
    combination/extension,
      brainstorming (usage), 112
    consideration, 119, 120
    creative ideas, allowance, 128–
      129
    cross-section, group
      representation, 32–33
    decisions, 120
    encouragement, 44–45, 176
    harvesting, brainstorming
      (usage), 112
    implementation, 121–122
    innovative ideas, allowance,
      128–129
    list, reduction, 121
    management approval, 122
    outside-the-box ideas, team
      offering, 41–43
    owner success, 121
    repetition, 41
    selection, 120–122
    stakeholder promotion, 186–187
    system improvement team
      development, 118
    team offering, 41–43
    usage, 40–41
Ideation, process, 112
IDEO, culture/work practices, 114
Implementation. *See* Change
    implementation
Improve, 84. *See also* Define,
    measure, analyze, improve,
    control
Improvement
    checklist, 138
    efforts, sabotage, 62

example, 134–135
initiatives, 177
opportunity, discovery, 12
optimal solutions, selection, 133
proof of concept budget,
    provision, 151–152
proof of concept, provision,
    151–152
seeking, 31, 34–35
solution selection, 5
solutions, tools/methodology
    (usage), 138, 150–151
Incremental innovation strategy, 116
Individual brainstorming, usage,
    113
Individual roles, impact, 62
Information
    cross-checking, 127
    non-traditional source, 26
    usage, 40–41
Innovation, 129
    culture
        encouragement, 182, 187–188
        system improvement team
            development, 118
    encouragement, 176
    importance, 41
    increase, 117
    requirements, 127
    strategies, types, 116–117
Innovative ideas, allowance, 128–
    129
Input, encouragement, 44–45
Interdependencies, types, 106
Internal customers, 36–37
In-the-know, examples, 15
Introverts, impact, 38
Inventory, 99
    bottleneck, impact
        (identification), 103
    definition, 104
    dollar impacts, 142, 143
    example, 139
    minimization, 105

Involuntary turnover, 57
Ishikawa, Kaoru, 76
Issues
    capture, brainstorming (usage),
        77
    root cause, study, 76

Jackson, Alan, 157, 159
Job camp, 116
Job Hazard Analyses (JHA), 75, 150
Job obsolescence, 74
Jobs, Steve, 35
Just-in-time delivery, 141

Kaizen, 75, 85–89, 150, 184
    intent, 86–87
Kanban, 85
Keenan, Perry, 157, 159
Key Performance Indicators (KPIs),
    53
Key process inputs, 84
Kim, W. Chan, 24, 128
Kitting process (Caterpillar), 128
Knowledge, spread, 114
Knudstorp, Jorgen Vig, 20, 46, 91,
    107–108, 131, 153
    guidance, 172

Labor-management relationships,
    improvement, 178
*Leader's Guide to Radical
    Management* (Denning), 148
Leadership, soft issue (focus), 159
Lean manufacturing, 179, 181
Lean practices, implementation, 180
Lean six sigma, 189–190
Lean thinking, 179
LEGO Case Studies, 12
    bottlenecks identification,
        107–108
    brainstorming, 131
    change implementation, 172
    continuous improvement, 191
    diversification, 107
    Future Lab, 131
    goals, identification, 63
    optimal solutions, 153

system improvement,
identification, 20
system observation, 91
team assembly, 46
Levitt, Theodore, 1
Line plots, usage, 84
Listeners, talking, 37–38

Management
buy-in, 11, 17–18, 186–187
change implementation buy-in,
138, 146
idea approval, 122
implementation role, 171
Margin, 104
Margin per FTE, 59
Marshall, Alfred, 136
Material throughput, improvement,
55
Mattel, 172
Mauborgne, Rene, 24, 128
Mead, Margaret, 157
Measure, 83. *See also* Define,
measure, analyze, improve,
control
Methods, Machines, Materials,
Manpower (4 Ms), 77
Metrics, 141
business goals, relationship, 53,
56–60
correctness, 123
challenge, 124
identification, 165–166
importance, 124, 187
organizational performance
metrics, 139
system performance metrics, 139
tracking, 165
usage, 53, 56–60, 164
Mistakes, fallout, 66–67
Money
measurement, 149
time, tradeoff, 137
Morale, improvement, 87
Motivation, soft issue (focus), 159

Motorola, statistical process control,
180
National Cash Register, CI program,
178
National cultures, conflicts, 44
Negativity
cessation, 129
reduction, 117

Objective bias, 88–89
Objective data, 125
Observation. *See* Stakeholders;
System observation
bias, absence, 88–89
organization/filing, 89
plan, system improvement team
leader approval, 68, 90
process, management, 67
simulation, creation, 87–88
team reliance, 100–101
visual representation, creation,
87–88
Ohno, Taiichi, 179
On-time delivery, 57
Open innovation strategy, 117
Operating expense, 99
bottleneck, impact
(identification), 103
definition, 104
dollar impacts, 142, 143
example, 139
minimization, 105
Optimal solution
definition, 10
form, 154–155
LEGO case study, 153
selection, 133
Organization
change, impact (analysis),
146–148
cultures, 175
conflicts, 44
shocks, types, 147
financial impacts, 133
process history, 115–116

profit, system improvement
(impact), 166–167
Organization (business goals), 49
changes, alignment, 125
changes, impact, 60
double-checking, 149–150
metrics, relationship, 166
Organizational gut-check,
performing, 145
Organizational metrics, usage, 139
Organizational performance
metrics, 139
Organizational productivity, 129
Organizational profitability,
business goal, 63
Organizational structure, transition,
189
Osborn, Alex, 113
Output
prioritization, 137–145
cost-benefit analysis, 149
profit, relationship (absence), 56
Outside-the-box ideas, team
offering, 41–43
Outside-the-box thinking, 130
Overestimated Value, 25
danger, 34
decisions/reversion, 30
elimination, 31
Ovesen, Jesper, 46, 91

Pain points, targeting, 167–168
Pareto charts, usage, 84
Passion, impact, 120
Past costs, increase, 12
Patient satisfaction, organizational
business goal, 54
Paycheck errors, 58
PDCA. *See* Plan, Do Check, Act
Peer Review group, discussions/
buy-in, 138, 145–146
Peer Review team, implementation
role, 171
Pentland, Alex "Sandy," 23–24
People, constraints, 102

Performance
business performance, 177
gap identification, 83
integrity, importance, 161
measurement, 187–188
metrics, tracking, 165
positive impact, 130
review/improvement, 187–188
Personal investment, provision, 87
Personal prejudice, 26
decisions/reversion, 30, 31
Pilot project, 152
Place, Procedure, People, Policies
(4 Ps), 77
Plan, Do Check, Act (PDCA), 86f
usage, 86
Planning system, improvement, 27
Policy, constraints, 102
PowerPoint presentation, usage, 71
Preliminary goal, definition, 18–19
Prioritization, cost-benefit analysis,
149
Problem
causes, listing/prioritization, 84
identification, 12
inclusion, 53
root cause, study, 76
solutions, identification
(purpose), 81
Process
documentation, 168–169
flow baseline, establishment, 83
inputs, impact, 84
mapping, 168
maps, 84
performance capability baseline,
creation (data collection), 83
process-based RCA, 78, 80
theory, 115–116
Production-based RCA, 80
Productivity, 104
group, brainstorming process,
126
improvement tools, 184–185

increase, 86
manager, impact (example), 166
stalemates, 123
Profit, 104
impact, 13–14
improvement, 56
output, relationship (absence), 56
understanding, 53
Progress, team tracking, 43
Projects
boundaries/scope, 83
impact, 149
metric, process performance
capability baseline
(creation), 83
pilot project, 152
project-based organizations,
project occurrences, 102
schedule, meeting/exceeding, 55
Project targets, 82, 83
Proof of concept
budget, provision, 151–152
prototype, development, 169
provision, 151–152
p-values, usage, 84

Qualified personnel, availability
(interdependency type), 106
Quality, 57, 59–60
business goal, 141
dollar impacts, 143, 144
impact, 13–14
improvement, 86
incident reports, 59
metrics, 141
understanding, 53
Quantitative research, usage, 66
Questions, correctness, 123
assumptions, 125

RCA. *See* Root cause analysis
Real Time Board, usage, 112
Recordables, 58
Relationships, network, 31, 40–41
Research, usage, 138, 150
Resistance, elimination, 74

Resources
allocation, 17–18
project competition,
interdependency type, 106
Respect, stakeholder promotion,
186–187
Results, analysis, 77
Retention, 50–51
Return on equity, 59
Return on investment (ROI), 59
analysis, 18, 36, 44, 122
break-even level, 145–146
calculation, 143
data, 167–168
expectation, 130
infeasibility, 168
profit, relationship, 51
solution, 135
tool, 24–25, 147
understanding, 138
Revenue
generation, 52
impact, 57
revenue per FTE, 59
Reward schemes, 178
Rework, reduction, 55
Ringen, Jonathan, 131
Risk
aversion, 129
reduction, 145
Robotics
cell, observations, 70
solution, example, 141–143
usage, 57
Root cause analysis (RCA), 75,
78–81, 88, 106
aim, 81
iterative process, 80
processes, 81
selection, 150
solution, 138
systematic performance, 81
types, 78, 80
usage, 103

Root causes
  correctness, identification, 125
  identification, 99, 103
  impact, 102–103
  prioritization, 84
ROS benchmarks, 172

Safety, 59
  business goal, 141
  dollar impacts, 142, 144
  goals, 137
  impact, 13–14
  improvement, 86
  metrics, 141
  safety-based RCA, 78
  training, 59
  understanding, 53
Safety-based RCA, 80
Sales, impact, 57
Scientific management, 178
Seidenberg, Ivan, 128–129
Shaw, George Bernard, 7
Sirkin, Harold L., 157, 159
Six Sigma, 82, 84, 180, 184
  approach, 181
Soft elements, 187
Soft issues, focus, 159
Software development, definition
    (usage), 151–152
South, Robert, 23
Staff, information/ideas, 40–41
Stakeholders
  answers, 125
  buy-in, 11, 17–18
  engagement, 67, 71–73
  impact, 90
  implementation role, 171
  non-operators, role, 72
  observation/communication, 67,
    74
Statistical process control, 180
Status quo, challenge, 31, 34–35
Stickiness factor, 183–184
Strategic planning/management
    system, 180

Structural productivity group,
    brainstorming process, 126
Subcontractors
  interdependency type, 106
  management, 72
Subject Matter Experts (SMEs),
    attendance, 40
Success
  definition, 81
  metrics, importance, 124
  team celebration, 32, 45
  track record, 171
Summary presentation, creation, 68,
    89
Surroundings, Suppliers, Systems,
    Skills (4 Ss), 77
Sutton, Robert, 112
  face-to-face brainstorms,
    guidelines (Sutton), 112–114
System
  bottlenecks, identification, 5, 12,
    93
  boundaries, 102
    identification, 14–15
  checklist, 11
  definition, 9
  example, 16
  financial impacts, accounting,
    140
  identification, 4, 7, 14
  interdependencies,
    understanding, 105–106
  performance
    impact, 130
    metrics, usage, 139
  personnel, involvement, 35–36
  processes, interdependencies
    (understanding), 105–106
System changes
  effort, leader role, 34
  impact, 60
    documentation, 168–169
    tracking, metrics
      (identification),
      165–166

measurement/tracking, 164
 cost-benefit, relationship,
  167–168
solutions, identification, 141
system improvement team
  tracking, 159
System improvement, 4, 7, 15
 achievement, 44–45
 analysis, 182–184
 goal, 105
 ideas, change (relationship), 124
 identification, 20
  form, 21
 impact, 13–14
 implementation, 137
 LEGO case study, 20
 preliminary goal, definition, 11,
  18–19
 problem, identification, 12
 research/analysis, completion,
  17
 time/resources, allocation, 17–18
System improvement goals
 impact, 105
 relationship, 53, 55–56
 setting, 62
 understanding, 62, 99
System improvement team
 culture, development, 117, 118
 engineer position, 71
 final selection, 122
 leader, 158
  group assembly, 31, 32–33
  observation plan approval, 68,
   90
  stakeholder/management
   selection, 11, 19
 members, origin, 120
 research/documentation, 45
System observation, 4, 11, 65
 analysis tool, usage, 74–87
 checklist, 67–68
 documentation, 67, 88
 example, 69

form, 92
LEGO case study, 91
organization/filing, 68
photos/videos, 67, 87
stakeholders, engagement, 71–73
summary presentation, creation,
 68, 89
Systems-based RCA, 78, 80

Talkers, listening, 37–38
TapRoot, usage, 103
Team
 action items, 39–40
 activity, 187–188
 agendas, 39–40
 bias avoidance, 117, 119–120
  impact, 127
 change implementation,
  accountability, 43
 contributions, preparation, 38–39
 culture, development, 117
 definition, 10
 disagreement/conflict/challenge,
  allowance, 32, 43–44
 echo chamber, avoidance, 31, 41
 failures
  allowance, 129
  impact, 32, 44–45
 form, example, 47
 ground rules, 39–40
 groupthink avoidance, 117, 123
  impact, 127
 ideas/alternatives, 31, 37–38
 innovation, increase, 117
  bias/groupthink, avoidance
   (impact), 127
 interaction, enjoyment, 45–46
 meetings
  holding, 31
  regular basis, 38–39
 progress, tracking, 43
 relationships network, 31
 success
  allowance, 129
  celebration, 32, 45

Team assembly, 4, 23
  checklist, 31–32
  example, 29–30
  LEGO case study, 46
Team leader
  change agent, 33–34
  meetings, 33–34
  responsibility, 32
  selection, 11
  stakeholder/management
    selection, 11, 19
Teamwork
  encouragement, 176
  mojo, 45
Technology
  aims, proof, 152
  definition, usage, 151
Theory of Constraints, 93–95, 184
  definitions, 104
  language, example, 107, 138–139
  usage, 103–104
Thoreau, Henry David, 111
Throughput, 56–57
  bottleneck, impact
    (identification), 103
  definition, 104
  dollar impacts, 142, 144
  example, 139
  improvement, 95
  maximization, 105
  metrics, 141
  rate, 99
Time
  allocation, 17–18
  money, tradeoff, 137
  studies, 138, 150
Timeline sequence (establishment),
    RCA (usage), 81
Tipping Point, The (Gladwell), 183
Total costs, examples, 143, 144
Total Productive Maintenance
    (TPM), 85
Total savings, 144

Toyota production system (TPS), 179
Toyota, success, 85
Training
  components, 159
  cost, increase, 142
"Training within Industry," 178
Trust, stakeholder promotion, 186–
    187
Turner, Ted, 128–129

Unsubstantiated data, basis, 121
Upstream boundaries, 140

Value
  overestimation, 25
    decisions/reversion, 30
  underestimation, 26
Velocity, 104
Vendors
  information/ideas, 40–41
  interdependency type, 106
  mismanagement, 72
Viseo, usage, 83
Visual representation, creation,
    87–88
Voice of the customer (VOC), 82
Voluntary turnover, 57

Warehouse, interdependency type,
    106
Welder manpower demands,
    reduction, 55
Welles, Orson, 124
Work
  performing, 146–147
  practices, brainstorming sessions
    (value), 113
Worker commitment, 162
Work in progress
  accumulation, 102
  backload, 60
  identification, 99
Workplace, improvement (employee
    rewards), 86

Zook, Chris, 46

About the Author

Joanna DeGeneres Photography

DORRIAH ROGERS BEGAN HER CAREER in the engineering and advanced technology industry in the late 1990s. She founded her consulting firm in 2003, and brings almost 20 years of unique experience providing guidance to numerous Fortune 100 and 500 organizations throughout North America. She specializes in identifying and solving issues affecting efficiency, productivity and profitability. Dr. Rogers approaches her clients strategically, with an eye toward management and project team efficacy, productivity and efficiency of operations, and financial streamlining. Her client base includes a who's who of Fortune 100 organizations, as well as the Department of Defense, U.S. Navy, U.S. Army Corps of Engineers, and other large government entities. As CEO of Paradyne Consulting Works, LLC, she has led her team in the areas of productivity and process improvement, strategic business planning, operational streamlining, profitability, and organizational change management. Executives find her insightful, candid, operationally savvy and a highly effective leader. She has earned the nickname "The Fixer" and has worked with many of her clients for more than a decade.

Prior to founding Paradyne Consulting Works, Dr. Rogers served as Chief Executive Officer, President and Chief Operating Officer for both private and publicly traded companies in the engineering, advanced technology and consulting fields. Her experience as an entrepreneur, technologist and executive has given her a unique and broad perspective from the ground up.

Dr. Rogers holds a PhD from the Graduate Group in Ecology, Institute of Transportation Studies from the University of California, Davis. She was appointed to the Ambassador's Club for the Society of Automotive Engineers, holds a patent for an emissions reduction technology, and also served on the National Academy of Science Transportation Research Board. She served as part-time faculty at California State University Channel Islands, where she taught Business Operations. Dr. Rogers has been named Entrepreneur of the Year and was nominated for Women Making a Difference, an award issued by the *Los Angeles Business Journal* in honor of women of outstanding achievement in the business community.